T0361237

SHIPPING IN TURKEY

This book is dedicated by the authors to Funda's grandfather - Huseyin Hilmi Celebioglu (1887-1959) - who was one of the pioneering master transport engineers in Turkey; and to Clive Mendonca for all his efforts on Monday May 25th, 1998.

Shipping in Turkey

FUNDA YERCAN
MICHAEL ROE
Institute of Marine Studies
University of Plymouth

Routledge
Taylor & Francis Group

LONDON AND NEW YORK

First published 1999 by Ashgate Publishing

Reissued 2018 by Routledge
2 Park Square, Milton Park, Abingdon, Oxon, OX14 4RN
711 Third Avenue, New York, NY 10017, USA

Routledge is an imprint of the Taylor & Francis Group, an informa business

A Library of Congress record exists under LC control number: 99072331

ISBN 13: 978-1-138-34836-3 (hbk)
ISBN 13: 978-0-429-43668-0 (ebk)

Contents

v

List of Figures

List of Tables

Acknowledgements

With two authors, acknowledgements are always difficult to organise as unlike the text they are not joint proposals but separate and specific to the individual. As a result these acknowledgements are divided into two parts, one for each of us.

Michael Roe
I would like to thank Marie Bendell at the Institute of Marine Studies for all her administrative help which has made final production of this text much easier than otherwise, and also Sarah Markham, Anne Keirby and Kate Trew at Ashgate for all their patience and good humour with another difficult academic. The trials and tribulations of Charlton Athletic have also helped (or perhaps hindered) progress with the text; and the continued support of Liz, Joe and Siân can never be overestimated. However, breaking all the rules about thanking co-authors, I would like to thank Funda most of all for her terrific dynamism and tenacity in seeing this research through to the end despite the enormous extra stresses of working in a foreign country and with both a young child and new baby. She has undoubtedly now become the leading expert in the maritime business sector in the East Mediterranean and it has been both a privilege and a pleasure to work with her. I look forward to doing so again in the near future.

Funda Yercan

First of all, I would like to take pleasure in acknowledging Michael Roe who was my supervisor during Doctoral studies at the Institute of Marine Studies, University of Plymouth and who in the preparation of this book gave great support. This involved a considerable number of email messages across Europe, giving immediate replies and solving problems. Additional thanks go to Dr Richard Gray who acted as second supervisor in the same department.

Many thanks to my parents, who encouraged me and took care of my daughters - Alemtac and Aysima - now aged 6 and 2 years, who paid in advance a heavy price for this work, and with whom I could not spend enough time as a mother when they needed me. Finally, my very special thanks are for my best friend and husband Ufuk, who has always encouraged me in my further studies.

Plymouth and Izmir, February 15th, 1999.

1. Introduction

Turkey has a long tradition as a maritime country with many centuries' history of ship operation and port activity, located as it is at the centre of early civilisation and the later developments of the economy of the Mediterranean. For these reasons alone it is surprising how little has been written about the Turkish maritime sector, which today in the 1990s represents a major industrial and commercial player in the region's economy.

This text hopes to address at least in part, this lack of material and has been derived from a detailed and extensive period of research conducted at the University of Plymouth, Institute of Marine Studies and led by Dr Funda Yercan, the leading maritime business expert in the region based at Dokuz Eylul University in Izmir, Turkey.

The maritime sector in Turkey is highly diverse and displays examples of all kinds of activity from bulk, liner and ferry shipping, through all types of port activity, to the ancillary sectors including broking, finance, law, agency and freight forwarding. It is an industry with some considerable history and one that lies central to political activity within the region. The most recent manifestation of this significance has come with the privatisation of the sector and the problems faced by the government in the remaining phases of transition with particular respect to the state shipping lines and the remaining state ports. Earlier phases of note have included the industry's relationship with the wider economy of Turkey and the problems faced by the ship building and ship repair sectors during the 1980s.

This text attempts to provide an analysis of each of the sectors of the Turkish maritime industry. However, it begins with an analysis of the country as a whole using as a basis a contextual model derived from the earlier work of Ledger and Roe (1996) which divides the significant issues and areas of

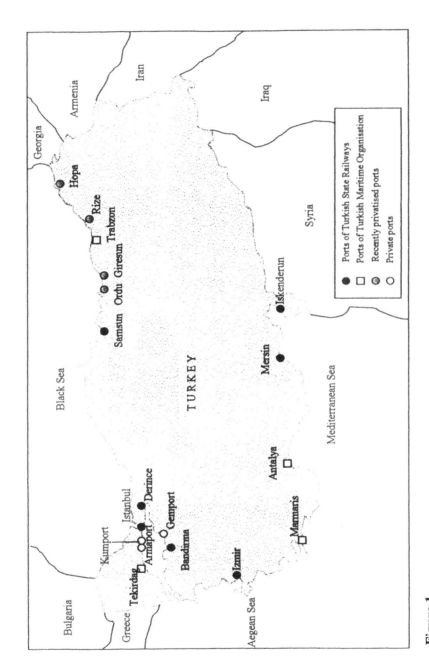

Figure 1
Major ports in Turkey

2

concern into a series of contexts for the convenience of analysis and then provides a discussion of their interrelationship.

Chapter Three goes on to provide an analysis of the shipping sector in particular since the liberalisation phases in the Turkish economy in the 1970s and 1980s and provides considerable original detail of the structure and importance of the sector and the major companies involved. Chapter Four provides a similar approach for Turkish ports.

Chapter Five looks at the ancillary sector with a review of activities such as finance and ship broking, agencies and freight forwarding whilst the next chapter takes the highly significant secondary shipping industry - that of ship building, repair and scrapping, which plays an important role in Turkey.

Finally Chapters 7 and 8 provide an analysis of shipping policy and that for the other associated sectors over the last few years and up to the turn of the century. A map to help the reader with basic spatial information is provided in Figure 1.

It is hoped by both authors that this text will provide a basis for further research into the region and will encourage others to go on and examine this fascinating sector. An extensive reference list is provided to encourage this activity. Anyone with further interests or enquiries is welcome to contact both of the authors at either institution (email *mroe@plymouth.ac.uk* or *yercans@unimedya.net.tr*) at any time.

2. Conceptual modelling for Turkish shipping; the conceptual contexts

Introduction

The role and significance of Turkish shipping in its broadest sense will be analysed in this section in some detail through the development of a model which adopts a qualitative approach. This approach has been preferred because it is the most appropriate way of dealing with the general principles that underlie the research using an exploratory process whilst explaining the problems and issues that may emerge both concisely and accurately. In so doing it provides a contextual framework for the more detailed explanation of the maritime industry which follows later in the text and which also provides for a discussion of the major issues.

The qualitative approach to modelling

The qualitative approach towards research modelling was developed considerably throughout the 1970s and since then has been widely used through the 1980s and into the 1990s. It is a relatively quick, normally cheaper, certainly more flexible and infinitely more adaptable approach in many circumstances compared with a quantitative approach towards the modelling of research problems and scenarios. The qualitative approach to research has been defined in many ways over the years but one reasonably comprehensive definition is:

> It answers questions such as 'What?', 'Why?' or 'How?' but it cannot answer the question 'How many?' It relies on interpretation of the findings of the data collection and allows access to the ways in which the respondents express themselves (Gordon and Langmaid, 1988).

A qualitative approach to research modelling tends to be characterised by the use of small samples and unconstructed data collection procedures. The techniques which are used normally develop an initial understanding of the issue in question in an exploratory way (Parasuraman, 1991) by attempting to provide a general review of the research context. The basic characteristics of this type of qualitative approach to research can be summarised as open-ended, dynamic and flexible, with a tendency towards the use of broader and deeper databases, providing in particular richer sources of ideas for marketing, whilst highly dependent upon research executive skills and providing results which help to increase understanding of the problem in hand (Gordon and Langmaid, 1988).

A qualitative approach is best used in analysing marketing problems where the results of the investigation and the interpretation of market conditions helps to increase understanding, expand knowledge, clarify the significant issues, explore and explain the market conditions, identify the behaviour of the supply and demand sides in the market area and provide input to further stages of the research. A qualitative approach to research modelling in this context is normally concerned with understanding the market rather than with measuring it.

The process of conceptual modelling is an essential part of all research but particularly in the qualitative approach adopted here, as it has been used to develop a database as a basic step for further analysis of the Turkish maritime industry. This technique is a more appropriate and effective way of analysing qualitative data rather than using conventional mathematical methods in the same way as explained by Ledger and Roe (1993). The model is operationalised through the contextual modelling process that follows next in this chapter.

Conceptual modelling

The process of conceptual modelling was chosen as the most appropriate and effective approach to help understand the contexts for the Turkish shipping industry using a qualitative approach to this research issue rather than traditional quantitative methods. The literature related to conceptual modelling is reviewed briefly in the next section to help provide a better understanding of what the model aims to achieve. Various applications of this model are summarised along with a specific example from the shipping industry. The model is then developed with particular reference to the Turkish shipping context and its application to the issues that are particularly important.

Literature that deals with conceptual modelling

The different approaches to the construction of a conceptual model, and the different stages through which it must pass can be specified in a number of ways, perhaps the most useful of which are indicated by the following:

> The use of real life information.
> Abstraction of the conceptual model from the real world.
> Developing a conceptual model, which is essentially qualitative in nature and approach.
> Conversion of the conceptual model to one which is quantitative in nature and which is suitable for use with the information and data values that the conceptual model was based upon.
> Operationalising the conceptual model in terms of conceptual contexts.
> Then proceeding to operationalise the quantitative model (Maddison, 1980).

A conceptual model represents the framework for manipulating the fundamental data required for the primary conceptual contexts which outline and present the boundaries to the significant issues within the research problem. They tend to be used in two ways, either to provide a set of structures for data and information so that this can be discussed and applied into the relevant research processes, or to form a starting point for the development of other models, which quite commonly will be of a quantitative nature.

Conceptual models are developed by revealing both the data needed to conduct the research and by analysing the research processes required. The terms used to describe these data and research processes in the conceptual model are as follows:

Data This can be described by entity, attribute or relationship. The distinction is made between entity or attribute in such a way that, 'entity' represents types of data and 'attribute' represents occurrences of data within the model. The relationships between data describe the meaningful associations that exist within the model.

Processes The ways the data is used is the process. Process can be represented by event, activity or operation. Here, commonly diagrams or written statements are used to represent the processes that take place in real life during the operationalisation of the model. For instance, conceptual contexts are the processes of a conceptual model, as they are the written statements that are based upon the data that emerges from the real life situation (Maddison, 1980).

Data models can be merged to form a wider ranging conceptual data model. In this case, entities and attributes, forming the data, are normally grouped together. A model structure is derived from the relationships between the data during the development of the conceptual data model. Conceptual process models are explained by many activities and operations, each of which can be thought of as a process. Consequently, conceptual modelling includes both of the above models, a conceptual data model and a conceptual process model.

Various applications of conceptual models can be found in the fields of computer science (Lindland et. al., 1994; Ryan, 1991; Meghini et. al., 1991; Crockett et. al. 1991; Sernadas and Carapuca, 1987), education (Giordan, 1991), engineering (Batra and Davis, 1992), human sciences (Batra, 1993), medical care (Wolinsky, 1994) and as a rare example, shipping. This latter is a particular conceptual model which provides an example from the shipping sector and was developed to analyse the economic, political and social changes that have occurred in Eastern Europe and their effects upon the maritime sector as a whole and the liner shipping industry more specifically (Ledger and Roe, 1993).

Developing the conceptual model

The conceptual model is developed below to give an explanation and provide the database for a qualitative approach towards the initial analysis of the Turkish shipping industry and to form the basis for understanding the Turkish shipping industry and related policy developments. The model is operationalised in the following section through a series of contexts which can be associated with the broad Turkish shipping industry. Thus, the developments and issues related to this subject are examined through the

7

various contexts within this model.

Operationalisation of the model: the contexts

The broad conceptual model developed to provide an initial analysis of the Turkish shipping industry was disaggregated into various sub-models which are explained in greater detail through operationalisation of the contextual framework outlined below. These contextual sub-models help to explain and indicate the major issues related to Turkish shipping.

Conceptual contexts

The conceptual contexts used to provide a framework for the contextual model of Turkish shipping are sub divided into spatial, political and historical, economic, social, technological, organisational and managerial, legal, marketing, logistical and environmental sections, and have been derived from the contextual sub-models developed previously for Eastern European shipping (Ledger and Roe, 1993). However, in addition, a marketing context was also developed as a consequence of the specific needs of this research and to reflect the review undertaken of other contexts.

Spatial context; the geographical situation and development of Turkey together with their effects upon the transport and shipping industries are discussed, in general, within this context.

Political and historical context; general history, political history, the current situation in the politics of Turkey and their effects upon the Turkish shipping industry are explained within this context.

Economic context; this context attempts to summarise the historical background to the Turkish economy, the recent economic development of Turkey, foreign trade relations of Turkey with the European Union and the relationship of all these sectors with Turkish shipping.

Social context; the relatively recent social changes that have taken place in Turkey which have had a significant impact upon the economic and political situation are based upon a broad policy of liberalisation. Their effect upon the Turkish maritime sector are specified within this context.

Technological context; the condition of technology generally within the Turkish shipping industry together with the specific technology used both at ports and in the shipping industry are summarised within this context.

Organisational and managerial context; this context considers the general structure of Turkish organisations related to and with an interest in the shipping industry and includes discussion of the issues of ownership and the internal managerial structures of the business as a whole.

Legal context; the position of Turkish Maritime Law in International Maritime Law together with the laws, regulations and issues of Turkish domestic Maritime Law where they relate to the maritime sector are discussed in general, within this context.

Marketing context; an overall summary and various details of the Turkish shipping industry in differing shipping markets are reviewed within this context in an attempt to place into a practical scenario the issues which emerge from the discussion of the other contexts.

Logistical context; the place of logistics and physical distribution in the transport sector and the Turkish maritime industry in particular, is explained within this context. A brief review of the development of intermodal transport and its relationship to the maritime sector, is also given.

Environmental context; the relatively rapid development and incorporation of the environmental approach within the maritime sector is discussed and a number of related issues are noted in this context.

The details of these contexts are fully explained in the following sections with particular reference to the Turkish maritime industry. It should be noted that there are some interconnections between the contexts and therefore some points are repeated whilst others show clear overlap.

Spatial context

The Republic of Turkey was founded in 1923 after the collapse of the 600-year-old Ottoman Empire. Modern Turkey is a developing and an industrialising country situated at a geographical position within the southeast of Europe, southwest of Asia, northwest of the Middle East and south of the Former Soviet Union, as noted earlier. Turkey has been commonly classified within different political categories as a consequence of its geographical situation, being considered both as a Middle Eastern country and a European country. However, the political and economic structures of Turkey are in many ways, different from those of the Middle Eastern countries. Furthermore, the only Islamic country with both a secular and a liberal political system has been Turkey. As a consequence, Turkey is considered a western country by those in the Middle East, a Middle Eastern country within Europe and an Islamic but a liberal, secular and western style democratic country.

Geography

Turkey consists of seven geographical regions: Marmara where the biggest metropolitan city Istanbul, is situated, Middle Anatolia where the capital and the second biggest metropolitan city Ankara, is situated, Aegean where the third biggest metropolitan city Izmir, is situated and the Mediterranean, Black Sea, East Anatolia and Southeast Anatolia regions. The northwest of the Marmara region is situated within the southeast corner of the European continent while the rest of the Marmara region and the other regions are situated in the very southwest of the Asian continent.

Middle, East and Southeast Anatolia regions are generally mountainous. The Black Sea, Marmara, Aegean and Mediterranean regions are named after the seas along which they have coasts. The result of this is that Turkey is situated in such a way that she has an approximate total of 8000 kilometres of coastline to the north, northwest, west and south. Civilisation, industrialisation and development have generally developed within the Marmara, Aegean and Mediterranean regions due to the ease of transport that derives from their maritime locations related to their spatial positioning.

Development

The volumes of both foreign and domestic trades and density of population are higher within the Marmara, Aegean and Mediterranean regions compared with the rest of the country. For instance, the current population of Istanbul in the Marmara region is 14 million, Izmir in the Aegean region is 4 million and Adana in the Mediterranean region is 2.5 million (SIS, 1996).

There has been a noticeable movement of people from rural areas to urban areas within the last thirty years, particularly from the eastern and south-eastern regions to the western and north-western regions. Therefore, the cities in the west and northwest have tended to be growing rapidly and have become full scale metropolitan cities. The major cities of Turkey shared some 46% of the total population in the late 1980s (OECD, 1988). The movement of people has been increasing rapidly due to the transformation of Turkey from an agricultural to an industrialised country which has stemmed from increasing industrialisation within certain regions.

Transport

The transport infrastructure has developed particularly within those strategic locations where industrialisation has prospered and continues to grow. As a consequence, most seaports have also been affected by this development. For instance, the Ports of Istanbul and Izmir traditionally have been the biggest ports both for exports and imports and are situated at the centre of all Turkish trade movements. The three ports of Turkey with the highest volume of external trades during the years 1990 to 1995 were the Port of Istanbul in the Marmara region, the Port of Izmir in the Aegean region and the Port of Mersin in the Mediterranean region (Mersin Chamber of Shipping, 1995).

Tourism

The Marmara, Aegean and Mediterranean regions have been the regions where tourism has been increasing as well as growing foreign and domestic trade volumes and industrialisation (Olali and Timur, 1992). The reasons for the growth are considered to be the historical and cultural structures that exist, and the combination of developments, monuments, ancient seaports and famous natural beauty spots situated along the sea coasts together with golden sands. As a consequence, the transport infrastructure has developed more in these regions compared with the rest of Turkey because of the growing volumes of both trade and tourism. For example, the most significant airports within Turkey are located at Ataturk airport (Istanbul) in Marmara, Esenboga airport (Ankara) in Middle Anatolia, A. Menderes airport (Izmir) and Dalaman airport (Mugla) in the Aegean region, and Antalya airport (Antalya) in the Mediterranean regions.

This growth of tourism has also been stimulated by the presence and growth of domestic ferry lines during the high tourism seasons. For instance, there has been substantial growth within the Istanbul-Izmir and Istanbul-Black Sea domestic ferry line corridors (TMO, 1993). Furthermore, both the Aegean and Mediterranean regions have become places for increasingly extensive yachting pursuits and cruise shipping activities during the summer seasons.

The external trade of Turkey has shown very rapid growth in exports since the early 1980s, particularly in terms of textiles, metals, foodstuffs and agricultural products. However, exports to the Middle East have fallen due to the substantial dropping of oil prices during 1986. On the other hand, there has been a rapid growth in imports since 1990 due to customs liberalisation and the Turkish expansion of import related markets (Europe Review, 1994). Therefore, the problem of an imbalance of external trade between exports and imports has now developed. However, there have been some attempts to close this imbalanced trade profile. One major attempt has been through tourism, whilst another has been through encouraging an increase in foreign currency brought to the country by Turkish people living and working in Europe. The savings of these Turkish people with currently an approximate population of 2.5 million (Yeni Asir, 1995) have been either transferred to their families living in Turkey or transferred for investment in Turkey every year. As a consequence, this input revenue helps to diminish the unbalanced external trade volume and to close the difference between the levels of exports and imports. Furthermore, some of these Turkish workers have developed into employers and investors within Europe during the past 20 years increasing their foreign earnings even further.

These Turkish people living and working in various European countries usually spend their summer holidays in Turkey and over many years in the past they have traditionally preferred to travel to Turkey by car following the roads of the former Yugoslavia and Bulgaria. The reasons for travelling by their own car were a preference for the flexibility that this affords both in Europe and in Turkey, the limited availability of rental cars in certain areas, the expensive prices of rental cars within the European countries, the desire to visit relatives and friends whilst en route which is a common, strong, cultural tradition in Turkey, the clear extra opportunities to carry additional personal belongings, and finally the difficulty of borrowing cars from local people for travel purposes because of the relatively small number of car owners in Turkey compared with the European countries (Dorsey and Hindle, 1995).

However, they have also started to travel to Turkey by the increasing number of charter flights that have been introduced over the last few years or by the developing and increasing number of ferry operations. These trends have been stimulated and encouraged by the war in the former Yugoslavia that developed from the beginning of the 1990s (TMO, 1993) and which continues to interrupt transport communications to this day. Therefore, the sizeable community of Turkish people living in Europe have started to play a vital role in the development of passenger ferry services within the Turkish shipping industry (TMO, 1994).

Consequently, the geographical situation of Turkey plays an important role in both domestic and international shipping movements. The geopolitical and strategic location of Turkey have direct impacts upon shipping particularly because of the range and quantity of transit movements between Europe and the Middle East (Lloyd's List, 1996c). In addition, industrialisation, development and increases in population that have taken place in the west and northwest of the country have also affected the shipping industry by stimulating direct increases in domestic and foreign trades, employment and education.

Recent developments within the transport sector in Turkey which have been seen in maritime transportation include the increasing development of seaports, the increase in external trade which is using sea transportation and increases in the volumes of passengers utilising domestic and international ferry lines. In addition, tourism has been concentrated upon the coastlines of Turkey and as such has affected the maritime industries through the development of yachting, cruise shipping and domestic and international ferry services. In particular and as we have already noted, the large numbers of Turkish people living in Europe have had a direct impact upon international ferry services in the Italy-Greece-Turkey corridor through their transport demands, predominantly occurring in the summer season. As a consequence, the international ferry services that operate in this corridor account for the majority of Turkish ferry services which are undertaking international services. As a consequence of all these developments, it should be noted that the Turkish shipping industry has been markedly affected by the significant developments and changes within the spatial context.

Political and historical context

A brief political history of Turkey

The major reforms and developments that the managers and politicians of the Ottoman Empire planned were put into action after the foundation of Republic of Turkey in 1923. These reforms took place during 1923-1933 under the presidency of Mr Ataturk. The main purpose of these reforms was to develop a new Republic with a western type life style, organisation, management and politics and represented a series of great changes, particularly in the political sphere after the traditions of the Ottoman Empire. For instance, some principal democratic rights, such as the right of women to vote and to be elected, were accepted within Turkey during the late 1920s and well before many European countries.

An authoritarian one-party regime ruled between 1923 until the 1940s. Turkey had a closed economy with no foreign relations during those years. A transition to competitive politics took place in the late 1940s after the end of World War II. Additionally, Turkey joined the United Nations and NATO in the 1950s as new steps in the development of diplomatic relations were taking place with other westernised countries. Further steps towards democracy were increased after the 1950s. Multi-political parties were developing and a more western political framework was adopted (Kurdas, 1994). Close external relations with Europe and the United States were built during that period.

Civilian governments were successively elected for approaching 32 years; however, military rule was also dominant for a period of six years at various times between 1950 and 1988. Military interventions took place in 1960, 1971 and 1980 due to political instability, the problems created by terrorist organisations of the extreme left, the Kurdish separatism issue and those stemming from the demands of the far right. Each of these periods were followed by periods of democracy (Sayari, 1992).

The current political situation of Turkey

The rapid growth of the Turkish economy, which had been taking place since 1983, started to slow down with the unfinished liberalisation policies of the Prime Ministry of Mrs Ciller. The Turkish Government started to adopt a strategy of total liberalisation policies together with privatisation as a cure for economic decline (Seatrade, 1993). In the meantime, the Government planned to develop more economic relations with European countries and to aid the economy in the long term with the Customs Union with the European Union, which was put into effect on 1st January 1996 (Lake, 1996).

Even though the development of Turkey was affected by the westernised politics that she applied for many years, this development did not help to increase the living standards of Turkish people in comparison with European countries. As a consequence, there has been a tendency for the domestic politics of Turkey to move against those in favour of westernising. The result was that the Welfare Party from the conservative movement and the Islamic wing was the leading party in the December 1995 general elections. A coalition was required to establish a new government which involved the leading and third parties with Mrs Ciller becoming the Deputy Prime Minister. However, instability in the political arena continued until another coalition between the Motherland Party and Republican Public Party was formed in 1997 moving the political wing to central left.

This instability and uncertainty in politics and economics has negatively affected steps towards a powerful, stable and encouraging future. The economic liberalisation movements since 1983, remained incomplete and the privatisation movement for state owned companies and institutions has been very slow (Observation, 1996). The privatisation programme, which has continued since the beginning of the 1990s, includes many maritime institutions, particularly the major four shipyards and three other small state owned shipyards situated in Istanbul and Izmir, a variety of ports and the cargo carrier - Turkish Cargo Lines, which is owned by Turkish Maritime Organisation (also the owner of the ferry operator - Turkish Maritime Lines) (Lloyd's List, 1994; LSM, 1994; Uysal and Mazgit, 1996).

The Turkish shipping sector and the political framework

The majority of the Turkish shipping sector lies within the private sector, particularly shipowners and ship operators and consequently, most Turkish shipowners, ship operators and shipyard owners have no little direct political impact and therefore, they have no direct effects upon elections and the distribution of votes. Their indirect political impact in particular, tends to take place through the Chamber of Shipping (Chamber of Shipping, 1996c). The chairman and members of the Board of Chamber of Shipping are the shipowners and ship operators. The major thrust of their indirect impact within the political sphere in recent years is to support the establishment of the Ministry of Shipping (Observation, 1996).

Currently, there is no Turkish Ministry of Shipping and all the maritime related institutions are under the responsibility of around ten Ministries of the Government. These include the Undersecretariat of Shipping, which is controlled by the Prime Ministry, and the Ministries of Transport and State, in particular. Moreover, the ongoing economic and political instability of the Government has tended to slow down the establishment of the Ministry of Shipping and, thus the development of the shipping industry (Chamber of Shipping, 1996b).

As a consequence, the instability that characterises Turkish politics has played a fundamental role within the shipping industry as well as many other industries. For instance, the establishment of a Ministry of Shipping has been a promise of a number of politicians since the beginning of the 1990s (Chamber of Shipping, 1996a). The heavy cuts in central budgets and the deficits in the total volume of foreign trades have negatively affected all economic sectors, including the maritime sector. However, the results of an economic package, put into effect in April 1994 with the aim of curing the economic decline, badly affected a large number of Turkish industrial sectors, although the shipping industry tended to benefit from the strategy because the sector depends upon hard currency earned by seaborne foreign trades and is little affected by the series of domestic economic crises that have occurred (Chamber of Shipping, 1996c).

Economic context

After many years of implementing inward-oriented economic policies, Turkey started to adopt a new outward-oriented model in its external economic relations from 1980 onwards. The two major elements of this model involved the liberalisation of foreign trade and the promotion of export-related activities. The structure of Turkey's foreign trade has undergone a substantial change through a seven-year implementation of this model leading up to 1987, during the Prime Ministry of Mr Ozal. Quotas and historical bans upon many import commodities were abolished, capital movements were freed and the foreign exchange regime was liberalised (Oyan, 1987; Togan *et. al.*, 1987).

Historical background to the Turkish economy

Both the developing and industrialising countries have traditionally protected their incipient manufacturing industries in the past when producing for their domestic markets. Turkey, as one of the developing countries, protected import substituting industries over exports and industry over agriculture during the period between 1950 and 1979. Turkey followed an inward-oriented development strategy during this period (Kazgan, 1985). The strategy was engaged until the mid-1960s, in replacing the imports of non-durable consumer goods, such as textiles, food processing etc, by domestically produced goods.

By the mid-1960s, Turkey was able to satisfy a large proportion of domestic demand for those commodities. There followed two choices for trading strategies and they were either to embark upon the exportation of manufactured goods, or moving on to the second stage of import substitution. Turkey chose a strategy of replacement of imports of intermediate goods, such as steel, refined products, petrochemicals etc, and consumer durables, such as vehicles, by those produced domestically (Togan *et. al.*, 1987). However, these commodities were highly capital intensive and required the availability of skilled and technical labour. A high level of protection of these industries was required and it was achieved through a system of tariffs, quotas and overvalued exchange rates. Accordingly, the incremental capital-output ratio increased considerably and eventually as a result, growth became more and more costly.

The Turkish economy grew steadily from the 1960s to 1973. Annual Gross National Product (GNP) growth between 1960 and 1969 averaged around 5.7%. The increase in GNP growth rate was achieved alongside modest inflation and healthy public finances. The rate of inflation by the GNP deflator averaged about 5.2% (SIS, 1995).

The strong growth performance of the Turkish economy during the 1960s was explained largely by the movement of labour from agriculture to industry and the high level of investment activity. The incremental capital-output ratio in manufacturing rose from 1.6 between 1963 and 1967 to 2.4 between 1968 and 1972. Similarly, the amount of investment per job achieved increased by 40% during the period 1963 to 1972 (SIS, 1980).

Between 1960 and 1969, exports increased at an annual rate of 6.1% in current US$ value. Over the same period, imports could only grow by 6.7% in current US$ value or approximately 3% in real terms compared with an average annual industrial growth rate of about 10%. Severe foreign exchange shortages were seen during the later half of the 1960s. Devaluation measures were introduced in 1970. Exports increased at an annual rate of 31.5% in current US$ value during the three years following the devaluation. GNP increased at an annual rate of 7.2% whilst inflation proceeded at an annual rate of 17.2% during the period of 1970 to 1973 (Togan *et.al.*, 1987).

The Turkish economy was affected by the quadrupling of oil prices between 1973 and 1974 and the world recession during 1974 to 1975. Turkey attempted to preserve its growth through rapid reserve decumulation and massive external borrowing. The successive governments refused to adapt their economic strategies to the new environment and they continued to pursue their expansionary policies. The investment programmes within the public sector grew sharply and the investment/GNP ratio increased from 19.1% in 1973 to 24.1% in 1977 (SIS, 1980). The gap between national savings and investment widened during the period of 1974 to 1976. The widening of the current account deficit developed into a payments crisis in 1977 and the spread between the Turkish domestic inflation rate and the worldwide inflation rate increased. These problems led Turkey to lose her international creditworthiness. The financial crisis forced Turkey to turn to the International Monetary Fund (IMF), and seek assistance from the OECD consortium.

In January 1980, the Turkish Government introduced a comprehensive policy package to correct the worsening of the economic situation. The immediate goals were to reduce inflation levels and balance the payments deficits. The budget deficit was reduced by widening the income tax base, raising some indirect tax rates and improving the tax collection procedures. After the military action that took place in September 1980, monetary policy was also tightened and actions were taken to increase the efficiency of the financial systems. A period of disorderly market conditions was followed by the freeing of interest rates at the beginning of 1981 (Oyan, 1989). The nine major banks were empowered to fix binding rates at regular intervals.

The recovery was spectacular in 1981, but the change in the Government in 1983 brought a relaxation of both the monetary and the budgetary measures. In December 1983, a new Government took power and a new policy package was introduced, by the Prime Minister Mr Ozal, with the aim of producing a greater degree of liberalisation. The new programme liberalised foreign trade and all goods could then be imported. Foreign exchange transactions were also liberalised. People could open foreign exchange accounts in banks or legally hold foreign currency. The authorities encouraged the emergence of strong and diversified trading companies. The trading companies with exports in excess of US$ 30 million in 1983, were entitled to access to special credit funds, duty free imports and foreign exchange. Impressive results were achieved during the period following the introduction of economic liberalisation. Between 1981 and 1986, the average real growth of GNP was 5.2%. Export growth increased enormously from around US$ 2.26 billion during 1970, to US$ 7.69 billion in 1985 (SIS, 1990).

Through the Prime Ministry of Mr Ozal in 1983, the Turkish economy was largely converted to a developing and internationally competitive industrialised and liberal economy. Turkey was brought into this new era where great changes in the political and economic environment were taking place. Mr Ozal's efforts to reshape the economy during the period from 1980 to 1993, took place in three different phases of political change. Firstly, economic policies, known as '24th January decisions' were formulated in 1980, under the 1980-1983 authoritarian military government. The policy of an outward-looking economy and growth based upon a free market economy was adopted. Secondly, with the Prime Ministry of Mr Ozal, Turkey started to move from military rule to limited political liberalisation between 1983 and 1987. Thirdly, a movement towards greater political openness and redemocratisation took place after 1987 (Sayari, 1992). Turkish politics were clearly markedly affected by these economic changes. This was a new era for the economic, political and structural development of Turkey and the liberalisation in the political economy was developed during the Ozal period (Oyan, 1989). A rapid growth for the whole economy and a growth in exports in particular, brought substantial and welcome credibility to Turkey within international markets.

Turkey had a long tradition of state controlled and inward-oriented economic strategies before Mr Ozal and liberalisation of the economy was a result of this new outward looking policy. In other words, Ozal's neoliberal strategy of economic growth, with an outward looking economy, represented a significant new phase for the development of Turkish politics and economics. Various reforms, such as tax policy, wages policy, monetary policy, privatisation plans and programmes, plans of forming a middle class and plans for forcing inflation down were developed during this period (Oyan, 1987; 1989).

New growing political and economic relations with the former Soviet Republics which had long standing Turkish connections started in 1991 after their independence (Kurdas, 1994), including Azerbaijan, Turkmenistan, Kazakhstan, Kyrgizstan, Tadjikestan and Uzbekistan in Caucasia and the Middle Asian region. Economic and cultural relations were initiated during this period, particularly, after signing the Black Sea Economic Cooperation Agreement between Turkey and many of these countries in addition to a number of others including Bulgaria and Romania. In this way, Turkey has played a pivotal role and is placed in a strong position for developing trading connections in the Black Sea area in the 1990s and through to the next century (Seatrade, 1993; LSM, 1994).

The effectiveness of the economic policies adopted has benefited greatly from the large scale foreign financial assistance during the initial period of the adjustment process, in particular. The most successful elements of the recovery were the growth of exports and certain services, such as construction, transport (including shipping) and tourism. Turkey tripled her merchandise export volume between 1980 and 1985. The country's share in total exports of non-oil developing countries to industrial countries increased from 0.9% in 1980, to 1.6% in 1985. At the same time the share of such exports to the Middle East countries increased from 4% in 1980, to 20.3% in 1985 (Kopits, 1986).

The importance of exports is considerable for the economic growth of Turkey. Export earnings enabled Turkey to import capital goods for the investment necessary for economic growth and to purchase the intermediate inputs required to keep the economy producing at its full potential. The transition of the economy from a bureaucratic system based upon restrictions and quotas to a liberal system operated with customs tariffs and free market conditions, reflected well upon the external reputation of the country. After the loss of international creditworthiness in 1977 due to the crises in balance of payments and increased exports, the process of regaining credibility began and was eventually achieved successfully.

Recent economic development of Turkey and liberalisation policy

A series of changes and measures was introduced within the stabilisation and liberalisation programme. This programme was supported by a number of international organisations such as the IMF, OECD and the World Bank. The liberalisation programme for the economy mainly constituted an outward looking and a free market oriented approach for Turkey. Targets of the programme included a strategy for reducing the high inflation rate, promoting exports, liberalising imports, liberalisation of foreign capital movements, reducing the role of the public sector in the economy by the privatisation of public sector enterprises and financial liberalisation for positive interest rates, an increase of domestic private savings and increase of circulation of money in the market (Uygur, 1993). In addition, some of the measures which were targeted, were establishing anti-inflationary monetary policy, fiscal policy, restoring competitiveness in external markets, exchange rate adjustments, stimulating trade liberalisation and improved market conditions (Nas, 1992).

Productivity was raised somewhat by liberalisation and export orientation because resources were used more intensively and more efficiently up to a certain limit stimulated by high competition. On the other hand, financial liberalisation could not totally raise the rate of private investment nor positively contribute to the rate of growth. These would only be possible if liberalisation has led to higher quality investments and a more efficient use of the capital stock that was available. The financial liberalisation that did occur, might have lead to significantly higher efficiency and higher productivity growth, but not sufficiently enough nor matching the expectations that had developed in Turkey.

Net effects of the liberalisation policy are hard to specify; however, it is possible to identify both positive and negative developments as a consequence of this policy for the Turkish economy. For instance, the GNP growth rate between 1980 and 1990, which was the most significantly liberalising period, and between 1960 and 1990 were approximately the same at an annual average of 5.4%. Thus, liberalisation has had positive impacts upon the Turkish economy in helping to stimulate a recovery in the 1980s, but it has not had the effect of raising the long-term growth rate of Turkey.

The liberalisation programme has not yet been successful in achieving its expected long term objectives as noted earlier. The objective of export growth was satisfied in general; however, import growth also increased resulting in an increase in the deficit between exports and imports in foreign trade (Uctum, 1992). Moreover, instability and uncertainty in the political cycles originating from Government policies or inaction in Turkey have had negative impacts upon the economy. Therefore, it should be pointed out that liberalisation cannot be a remedy for disequilibria that result from governmental policies and political economic models. An explanation for the lack of total success in the liberalisation policy in Turkey was suggested by Uctum (1992) who claimed that the liberalisation programme has coincided with the stabilisation programme; however, the economy should have been stabilised first before it was liberalised and lessons should have been taken from the experience of South American countries.

Thus, liberalisation can be a more efficient, advantageous and cooperative tool for the Turkish economy in the long term if a stable and a credible political situation free from uncertainties exists. In addition, free market oriented growth in Turkey could be an important source of stimulus for improved economic efficiency. Stabilisation, structural adjustment reforms and liberalisation would be more effective enabling the economy to achieve macroeconomic objectives. On the contrary, the liberalisation policy in Turkey still has some positive effects upon the economy even during the current unstable and uncertain political situation based most probably upon the dynamics of Turkey's unique economic environment during this transition period.

During the Prime Ministry of Mr Ozal after 1983, the statistics started to be impressive as a result of the liberalisation processes going on within the Turkish economy. The liberalisation policy proceeded as following:

> Providing for foreign capital the same rights and obligations of domestic capital with guarantees given in transferring profits.
> The recognition of the Foreign Investment Directorate as the single authority in Turkey, which guides, receives, reviews and negotiates all foreign investment applications.
> The encouraging results of foreign capital flowing towards Turkey. Whilst the cumulative foreign capital inflow was US$ 228 million between 1954 and 1980, the same inflow proved to be US$ 364 million in 1986, alone.
> The Gross National Product/per capita more than doubled from US$ 1,280 to US$ 2,700 in 1992 after massive exports from the country.

A new middle class was formed and foreign capital was brought in to take advantage of a growing domestic market. In addition to these developments, the introduction of free trade zones also started to attract a number of foreign investors to Turkey. There were more than 2,600 foreign companies operating in the country during mid-1994. 54% of these companies were operating in the manufacturing industry sector, 43% in the services sector and 3% in other sectors (Lloyd's List, 1994). Exports nearly tripled from US$ 5.7 billion to US$ 15.3 billion per annum; however, imports also tripled from US$ 10 billion to US$ 29.4 billion per annum, by the end of 1993. Annual inflation dropped from around 66.1% to 70.1% by the end of the same year.

The domestic industries in Turkey have started to display an international competitiveness and have an increasing comparative advantage for exports in agriculture and livestock, mining and quarrying products, textiles and clothing, ceramics and iron and steel, compared with the past.

Turkey signed an agreement, called the 'Black Sea Economic Cooperation' in 1992 with the Turkish republics, also known as the Turkic republics, on the north Black Sea shore and in Central Asia. These countries included Azerbaijan, Turkmenistan, Kazakhstan, Kyrgizstan, Tadjikestan and Uzbekistan. As we noted earlier, Turkey in terms of geography, is a European but also an Asian, a Middle Eastern, a Levantine and even a Balkan country having substantial potential for strong economic relations with a wide variety of countries within the region (Financial Times, 1994). Turkey is thus designated as:

> a potential regional hub for world trade with the new
> democracies of Eastern Europe, the Turkic republics of Central
> Asia and the littoral states of the Black Sea, (Lloyd's List, 1994).

However, the economy of Turkey was running out of control during the Prime Ministry of Mrs Ciller and after the sudden death of President Mr Ozal at the beginning of 1993. An overvalued Turkish Lira and high consumer demand lead to a massive increase in the trade deficit. Turkey was growing quickly, but the growing rate of population was also increasing quickly. Therefore, the rate of increase of national revenue per capita was not enough to keep pace. Furthermore, economic instability stemming from the growing rate of growth of the country was obvious during the late 1980s and early 1990s. For instance, whilst the growth rate in terms of GNP was 1.9% in 1989, it rocketed to 9.4% in 1990, followed by a rate of 0.3% in 1991, then 6.4% in 1992, 7.3% in 1993 and -6.0% in 1994 (Ersoy and Guran, 1993; Europe Review, 1994; SIS, 1995). The main economic indicators of Turkey are illustrated in Table 1. Following a review of the recent economic situation in the middle of the 1990s the following characteristics of economic strategy could be identified:

> The Treasury heavily relied upon Central Bank resources in the second half of 1993.
>
> Macroeconomic imbalances and the decline in Turkey's credit rating led to a crisis situation in the second half of 1994.
>
> Strong pressure on exchange rates led to a substantial depreciation in Turkish Lira.
>
> Financial markets remained highly volatile.
>
> A stabilisation programme was enforced in the middle of 1994.

Table 1
Main economic indicators of Turkey (1990-1995)

	1990	1991	1992	1993	1994	1995
GNP (US$ bn)	150.8	150.2	158.1	178.7	132.8	99.2
GNP per capita (US$)	2,682	2,620	2,707	3,004	2,193	2,758
Index of internal purchasing power (base 1990 = 100)	100	60	35	21	10	n.a.
Index of external purchasing power (base 1990 = 100)	100	59	39	25	23	n.a.
Inflation rate (annual %)	52.3	55.3	62.1	58.8	120.7	64.9
Wholesale price index change (%)	52.2	55.3	62.1	58.0	137.6	77.3
RPI change (%)	60.3	66	70.1	66.1	115.8	84.4
Manufacturing prodn. index change (%)	9.5	1.8	4.2	9.4	-4.2	2.7
Unemployment (% total labour force)	8.2	7.9	7.9	7.6	11.1	10.7
Interest rate	47.6	68.4	72.8	67.1	105.2	94.8
Value of exports (FOB) (US$ bn)	13.0	13.6	14.7	15.3	18.1	21.6
Value of imports (CIF) (US$ bn)	22.3	21.0	22.9	29.4	23.3	35.7
Trade balance (US$ billion)	-9.3	-7.4	-8.2	-14.1	-5.2	-14.1

n.a.: not available
Sources: European Marketing Pocket Book 1994 (1995); AIIB (1996); AITB (1995), (1996).

23

Structural reforms and tight monetary fiscal policies were on
the agenda.
Markets were stable in the first half of 1995.
Some reasonable success was achieved in 1994 as a result of
tight monetary policies and structural reforms (ATIB, 1995).

It is clear from Table 1 that Turkey is a developing country with low values
for many of its economic indicators. The total annual value of exports and
imports over the period between 1990 and 1995 is illustrated separately in
Table 2. It is notable that the total value of trades declined in 1994
whencompared with the value in 1993 although it increased again in 1995.

The Turkish economy was dominated in 1994 by efforts to recover from the
financial currency crisis in January. State owned companies of the public
sector were the root cause of the financial crisis, and the estimate of the cost
of the crisis to the economy was approximately US$ 4.7 billion for 1995. The
crisis caused the economy to shrink to 6% in GNP real growth terms in 1994,
whilst it had been 7.3% in 1993 (Europe Review, 1994). GNP per capita
dropped to US$ 2,193 in 1994, from a figure of US$ 3,004 in 1993 (Europe
Review, 1995). Additionally, the annual average inflation rate for 1994 was
120.7%, sometimes even reaching 139% (Lloyd's List, 1994) and peaking at
146.7% (AAYB, 1995), thus eating into the living standards of every Turkish
person. The Turkish Lira was devalued by 15% and the US dollar exchange
rate against the Turkish Lira was up by 100% in the first four months of 1994.

Table 2
Turkish foreign trade between 1990-1995 (US$ billion)

	1990	1991	1992	1993	1994	1995
Exports	13.0	13.6	14.7	15.3	18.1	21.6
Imports	22.3	21.0	22.9	29.4	23.3	35.7
Difference (+:surplus, - :deficit)	-9.3	-7.4	-8.2	-14.1	-5.2	-14.1
Total trade volume	35.3	34.6	37.6	44.7	41.4	57.3

Sources Containerisation International (1995); SIS (1995); SIS (1996).

Interest rates also increased to more than 10% a month and there developed
the tendency for people to keep their money rather than use it.

An ambitious rescue plan was unveiled by Mrs Ciller on 5 April 1994. This
plan provided a structural programme for price increases on many state

monopoly goods, the imposition of a one-off low rate tax, acceleration of the privatisation programme, plans to grant autonomy to the Central Bank to free it from financing the budget deficit, and a stabilisation programme for the economy. After one year of operating this economic package, the general feeling was that it had been only moderately successful. The main objective of the package was to bring macroeconomic stabilisation to the Turkish economy; however, it has not been achieved and the economy was still shrinking.

Turkey's chronic debt problem continued in 1994 and early 1995. The country's total external debt increased by 2.6% in nominal terms in 1994 to US$ 65.6 billion. The trade deficit, which illustrates the difference between exports and imports, was approximately US$ 5 billion in 1994. Some negotiations with the IMF were in progress for borrowing some money to finance the deficits, and a six-month loan was agreed in July 1994. The fund initialled a second loan providing US$ 157 million in stand-by loans in April 1995.

The current economic situation of Turkey

Turkey has adopted the policy of a liberal economy in the 1980s as noted earlier. The government was separated from the policy of a mixed economy, where decision-making is a function of both the government and the market. The government has continued the policy of developing an outward looking and liberal economy. Freedom in the use of foreign currency and its retention in bank accounts were maintained as a result of the liberalisation policy applied to the economy. Therefore, the Turkish Lira was considered as a fully convertible currency until the economic crisis that took place in April 1994. However, following that time it is clear that the Turkish Lira became to be considered as an unstable and in some ways valueless currency compared to hard currencies, particularly the US dollar, DM, Sterling and Japanese Yen due to the high domestic inflation rate stemming from the instability of the economic, political and social situation. However, the convertibility of the Turkish Lira has now been restored as a result of the decline in the annual inflation rate and the increasing stability of the economic situation.

Meanwhile, the Turkish Central Bank has been the biggest power affecting the foreign currency markets. These effects have influenced the politics of the general domestic economy, domestic interest rates, and the policies of exports and imports applied by the Government.

Exports increased from US$ 18.1 billion in 1994, to US$ 21.6 billion in 1995. Additionally, imports increased from US$ 23.3 billion in 1994 to US$

35.7 billion in 1995. As a consequence, the trade deficit nearly tripled from US$ 5.2 billion in 1994, to US$ 14.1 billion in 1995 (AIIB, 1996; SIS, 1996). These developments are illustrated in Table 2.

The State Planning Organisation published the seventh Five Year Plan for Development for the years 1996-2000, in May 1995. The plan envisaged a decline in annual inflation of 6% and minimum annual growth rates of 8.1%, based upon the successful progress of the EU customs union, increased privatisation of state owned companies and institutions, taxation reform and a reconstruction programme in the southeast region of Turkey, known as "The Southeast Anatolia Project" (Europe Review, 1995; State Planning Organisation, 1996). The development plan also proposed new developments for trade relationships between Turkey and the European Union, the Islamic countries, the Turkish Republics in Caucasia and Central Asia and the countries which are part of the Black Sea Economic Cooperation community (Temel, 1996).

Despite the economic and institutional reforms over the past few years, which have been intended to make the country more attractive to foreign investors, Turkey is not yet in a position to take advantage of its reforms. Foreign investors still suffer (or feel that they may suffer) from shortcomings in terms of economic and political instability. Turkey can attract foreign investment and benefit from it as long as it remains a relatively open and stable economy compared to many other developing countries against which she is in strict competition.

Foreign trade relations of Turkey with the European Union

A major development in the European Union (EU) affecting the Turkish economy has been the Union's south-eastern enlargement into the Mediterranean region during the beginning of the 1980s. The impact of this enlargement upon the Turkish economy for exports reveals that Turkey has to compete with Greece and Portugal, particularly in textiles, whilst Spain seems to be a much more important competitor in agricultural products, such as vegetables and fresh fruit. Turkey has a comparative advantage vis a vis the EU in textiles, leather, vegetables, fresh fruit, prepared foodstuffs and glass.

Turkey's foreign trade with the EU consisted of total exports fluctuating between 49% and 38% during the 1980s, and imports from the EU which varied between 28% and 41% (Togan *et.al.*, 1987). The growth of exports to the EU has been explained largely by the changes in cost competitiveness that have occurred and by the growth in real incomes in the EU. The 1979-1986 period exhibited considerable improvement in trade relations between Turkey

26

and the EU. Exports to the EU increased continuously and so did imports from the Union with the new export-oriented policies since 1980. Between 1983-1984, exports measured in current US$ increased very sharply by about 35.9% (SIS, 1990). However during the period between 1984 and 1985, the rate of increase of exports dropped to 15% per annum. Despite absolute decreases in overall exports in 1983 and 1986, Turkish exports to the EU continued to increase. Meanwhile, Turkish textile exports to the EU have recovered. In 1987, customs duties on imports of agricultural products from Turkey were eliminated. The imports of Turkey from the EU increased quickly between 1983 and 1986 and the trade deficit, which was narrowing until 1984, started to widen considerably.

The increase in the exports of Turkey to the EU during the period between 1990 and 1994, was approximately 20%. The amount of exports to the EU increased from US$ 6.906 billion in 1990 to US$ 8.269 billion in 1994. The percentage of exports to EU countries was 46% of the other country groups to which the total Turkish exports were made in 1994 (SIS, 1995). Similarly, there was an increase in the imports to Turkey from the EU of 10.3% during the period 1990-1994. The quantity of imports from the EU was US$ 9.354 billion in 1990 and increased to US$ 10.279 billion in 1994. The percentage of imports from the EU was 43.6% of the other country groups from which total Turkish imports originated during this period (SIS, 1995).

The total amount of exports of Turkey to the EU countries was US$ 11.078 billion, whilst the total amount of imports from the EU countries to Turkey was US$ 16.861 billion in 1995 (SIS, 1996). The total amount of exports of Turkey to the EU countries in comparison with the other countries, i.e. the OECD, Islamic, Middle Eastern, Gulf, North African, OPEC and other European countries, during the period between 1990 and 1995 is illustrated in Table 3. The percentage of total exports from Turkey to the EU countries in comparison with the other countries was 51% in 1995.

The total amount of imports from the EU countries in comparison with the other countries during the period 1990-1995 is illustrated in Table 4. The percentage of the total amount of imports from the EU countries in comparison with other countries was 47% of US$ 35.709 billion in 1995.

Table 5 illustrates the top ten countries to which Turkey exported in 1994 and 1995. The percentage of each country in the total exports of Turkey is also illustrated in the table. Similarly, Table 6 illustrates the top ten countries with which Turkey had trade relations for imports in 1994 and 1995.

Table 3
Total amount of exports from Turkey to the EU countries in comparison with other countries between 1990-1995 (US$ billion)

	1990	1991	1992	1993	1994	1995
EU countries (*)	6.906	7.042	7.602	7.289	8.269	11.078
Other European countries	1.145	1.284	1.474	1.953	2.435	3.561
OECD countries	8.823	8.857	9.354	9.068	10.740	13.215
Islamic countries	2.323	2.729	2.778	2.805	3.047	3.265
Middle Eastern countries	1.629	1.850	1.972	1.989	2.108	2.132
Gulf countries	1.230	1.196	1.340	1.364	1.346	1.209
North African countries	0.648	0.692	0.637	0.597	0.725	0.900
OPEC countries	1.668	1.667	1.711	1.696	1.816	1.759
Total exports	**12.959**	**13.594**	**14.719**	**15.348**	**18.105**	**21.636**

*: EU comprised 12 countries until 1994, and 15 countries from 1995
Source: SIS (1996).

Referring to Table 5, eight European Union countries were in the top ten countries with which Turkey had trade relations in terms of exports both in 1994 and 1995. Seven EU countries were in the top ten countries from which Turkey imported goods in 1994 and 1995, as illustrated in Table 6. Germany was the top country with which Turkey had both exports and imports relations in 1994 and 1995.

As is reasonably clear from Tables 3 to 6, the trade relations of Turkey with the European Union countries play an important role within the total foreign trade scenario and in terms of the economic integration of Turkey with the world trades. 51% of Turkish exports and 47% of imports were undertaken with the EU countries in 1995 (SIS, 1996). Therefore, speeding up trade relations with the EU has always been a priority for Turkey whilst maintaining foreign trades also with many other countries, such as those of the Middle East, the Gulf region, the Islamic countries and the Turkish Republics in Caucasia and Middle Asia.

Table 4

Total amount of imports to Turkey from the EU countries in comparison with other countries between 1990-1995 (US$ billion)

	1990	1991	1992	1993	1994	1995
EU countries (*)	9.354	9.222	10.049	12.950	10.279	16.681
Other European countries	2.218	2.030	2.226	3.359	2.590	4.553
OECD countries	14.251	14.071	15.421	19.975	15.312	3.511
Islamic countries	3.854	3.183	3.414	3.518	3.355	4.315
Middle Eastern countries	2.706	2.491	2.648	2.799	2.530	2.687
Gulf countries	2.518	2.302	2.468	2.577	2.338	2.220
North African countries	0.938	0.481	0.575	0.381	0.628	1.143
OPEC countries	3.338	2.681	2.980	2.836	2.839	3.230
Total imports	**22.302**	**21.047**	**22.870**	**29.429**	**23.270**	**25.708**

*: EU comprised 12 countries until 1994 and 15 countries from 1995
Source: SIS (1996).

Following our discussion of the disadvantageous points of the Turkish economy, it is necessary to emphasise that Turkey will benefit from the customs union with the EU in the long term and most probably improve its economic stability together with the steps planned, by the seventh Five-Year Development Plan. The total amount of exports, imports, and therefore the total volume of foreign trade of Turkey with the European Union countries are expected to increase in the near future based upon the free movement of goods between Turkey and the EU resulting from the Customs Union, which was put into action on 1st January 1996 (Lake, 1996). Transportation and shipping in particular, appear to be gaining more importance during the integration period with the EU and after the Customs Union. Since maritime transportation is the most common and significant way of transporting goods throughout the world and approximately 95% of world trade is carried by sea transport, shipping and sea transportation is likely to be highly important for the increasing trade volumes between Turkey and the EU.

Furthermore, it is also clear that economic indicators of increasing exports and imports and a stable economy both directly affect the shipping industry as

Table 5

Top ten countries for exports from Turkey (1994-1995) (US$ bn)

	1994	1995	change (%)
Germany	3.934	5.036	28.0
U.S.A.	1.520	1.514	-0.4
Italy	1.034	1.457	40.9
Russian Federation	0.820	1.238	51.0
United Kingdom	0.889	1.136	27.8
France	0.851	1.033	21.4
Netherlands	0.621	0.737	18.7
Saudi Arabia	0.609	0.470	-22.8
Belgium & Luxembourg	0.371	0.452	21.8
Spain	0.232	0.354	52.6
Total 10 countries	**10.881**	**13.427**	**23.4**
Total exports	**18.105**	**21.636**	**19.5**
Total 10 countries / total exports	**60%**	**62%**	-

Source: SIS (1996)

Table 6

Top ten countries for imports to Turkey (1994-1995) (US$ bn)

	1994	1995	change (%)
Germany	3.646	5.548	52.2
USA	2.429	3.724	53.3
Italy	2.009	3.193	58.9
Russian Federation	1.045	2.082	99.2
France	1.458	1.996	36.9
United Kingdom	1.170	1.830	56.4
Japan	0.968	1.400	44.6
Saudi Arabia	1.229	1.383	12.58
Netherlands	0.740	1.084	46.5
Belgium & Luxembourg	0.532	0.912	71.4
Total 10 countries	**15.226**	**23.152**	**52.1**
Total imports	**23.270**	**35.708**	**53.5**
Total 10 countries/ total imports	**65%**	**82%**	-

Source: SIS (1996)

well as other industries in the country. Additionally, a generally improving economy for Turkey would positively and directly affect the Turkish shipping industry. As a consequence, it becomes necessary for Turkey to continue the improvements to the economy for many industries but for the shipping industry in particular. The shipping industry is a rapidly growing and developing industry with an increasing contribution to make to the Turkish economy. As a result of both improving and increasing trade relations with the EU, the shipping industry has been markedly affected and will continue to be affected by these developments but will also make its own contribution back to the economic development of the country itself, having substantial positive effects many details of which will be explained later in this text.

Social context

The strong and far reaching liberalisation policy characteristic of the outward growing Turkish economy has had a large number of varied social consequences. There is a marked division between urban and rural inhabitants that clearly differentiates the social characteristics of the Turkish population. Education, dress, outlook, traditions and wealth are the main elements that substantiate these social characteristics. Cities are the home of Turkey's western-educated, modern and elite people, who provide the general direction for the Government. People living in the rural areas are engaged mainly in agriculture (Middle East Research Institute, 1985). Urban and educated women have achieved impressive access to professional life. Economic necessity and increasing educational levels have combined to encourage many women into different careers, as well as business and politics.

Turkey is rapidly becoming urbanised due to the growth of the centres of industrialisation. Over 75% of the country was rural in the 1950s; however, the annual change in urban population was 5% in 1985 whilst the annual rate of natural population increase was 2.2% (OECD, 1988). Furthermore, the percentage that cities held in terms of total population was approximately 65% and the annual growth rate of these cities was 4.3% in 1995 (Buyukdeniz, 1996). On the other hand, the proportion of rural population was 35% and the annual growth rate in rural areas was -6% in the same year. Istanbul in the Marmara region, Ankara in the Central Anatolia region and Izmir in the Aegean region, as the largest cities, have become the strongest magnets for migration from rural areas (Yalcintas, 1996).

This movement of people from the rural areas to the industrialising and developing urban areas causes various problems, such as an increase in recession and unemployment. Social pressures have also increased on the people living in the cities with large numbers of uneducated and lower qualified people settling in the surrounding areas of the major cities. These people directly affect the increases in unemployment and problems arising from housing, transportation, infrastructure, education, healthcare and environmental protection (Ozturk, 1996). These also have some direct and indirect effects upon employment in the shipping industry.

In addition to these social issues, the indicators related to education emphasise the lack of higher education. Only 26.7% of the total population completed higher education while 53% completed secondary school in 1994 (Buyukdeniz, 1996). These indicators also have both various direct and indirect effects upon the shipping industry because the lack of higher education and maritime schools and faculties in Turkey is beginning to cause substantial problems for the industry in meeting its seafarer and officer needs for the merchant fleet.

The progressively fierce competition rules, with increasing foreign investment and capital, based upon free market conditions have had some impacts upon employment. Unemployment rates have been increasing particularly for low qualified people in various fields because the market is a rapidly growing dynamic market based upon high competition and thus requiring the highest of standards along with the minimum of labour force. Additionally, the rapid increase in the total population with an annual rate of 2% in 1994 plus some 62.5% of the total population who are of workforce age (i.e. 15-64) (State Planning Organisation, 1995) have both had serious impacts upon the notable increase of unemployment. Although there is a form of social insurance for working people, unfortunately, there is still no unemployment insurance for those without work (Uslu, 1996).

In addition to these issues, high inflation with an average annual rate of 86% in 1995 (SIS, 1996) is one of the other major disadvantageous effects of the economy upon social life in Turkey. The purchasing power of people is continuing to get smaller every day and thus is eating away at the welfare of the society. The annual average net income per capita was US$ 2,193 in 1994 (ATIB, 1995). This amount decreased to only US$ 529 for the poorest grouping, which represents some 20% of the population. In addition a decrease to US$ 1,448 in the middle division was also noted, which represents 60% of the population. Meanwhile, the figure increased to US$ 5,932 in the richest division, representing only 20% of the population, in 1994 (Hurriyet, 1996).

The growth rates of private final consumption expenditure decreased from 8.4% in 1993 to -5.3% in 1994 because of the economic crisis in Turkey;

however, it recovered and again increased to 7.6% in 1995. These economic indicators also reflect the social life of the Turkish people because of the strong ties that exist between economic and social issues. These indicators include the annual growth rates of consumption of food, beverages, durable goods, semi-durable and non-durable goods, energy, transportation, communications, services and ownership of dwellings.

In addition, the Turkish economy was in crisis in 1994 as we have noted earlier. The annual average inflation rate was 116% in 1994 (AAYB, 1995). Employment was highly affected by the crisis and the annual rate of unemployment was 11.1% in urban areas and 5.1% in rural areas in that same year (AIIB, 1996). As a result of this situation in the economy, employment in the state sector of the shipping industry was affected. The shipyard workers in particular, felt the pressures that these economic conditions placed upon the labour market place and the unions of these workers attempted to protect the rights of the workers against low wages and job losses. However, the economic crisis in Turkey did not affect the private sector of the shipping industry as directly as the state owned sector because of the opportunities afforded to the shipping staff as well as the industry more generally, to earn hard currency.

Social issues such as the high rate of population increase and the high rate of migration from rural areas to urban areas have had direct effects upon various issues, particularly unemployment, housing, transportation and education. These also affect indirectly the state owned shipping industry through their knock-on impact in terms of issues such as spending power, mobility, accessibility and the demand for increased incomes.

The free market reforms introduced by Mr Ozal in the 1980s have led to a changeable period and a new stage of development for Turkey as we noted earlier. These reforms have had many and various social impacts and still continue to have a major effect within Turkey. The liberalisation policy as part of the free market initiative affected the Turkish shipping industry as much as most other industries, including those of banking, manufacturing and the automotive sector. In fact many shipping companies have been reflecting this transformation stage of Turkey's economic, political and social history since the mid 1980s. During this time, the traditional Turkish shipping company has developed from the historic and traditional maritime enterprise of the Ottoman Empire to a dynamic, growing and modern sector. Shipowners have been affected by these social changes, stemming from the liberalisation policy, by becoming more active and by taking a collective approach to develop and improve the industry.

Turkey's financial liberalisation policy increased the degree of monetisation in the financial system, raised the short term indebtedness of the public sector and caused an erosion in private wealth by accelerating real asset liquidation (Akyuz, 1989). In this framework, the erosion in wealth has started to cause a growing difference between the social welfare within segments in the private society.

As a result of the outward growing and liberalisation policies in the Turkish economy and political scene and in addition the Customs Union that has been agreed with the EU, there has been and will continue to be, major social impacts upon the Turkish shipping industry.

Technological context

This context concentrates upon a review of the technological level of the infrastructure within maritime companies, institutions and establishments in Turkey. The total Turkish merchant fleet amounted to 10.31 million dwt with an average age of 18.4 years at the end of 1995 and had reached 10.89 million dwt and an age of 17 years at the end of 1996 (Chamber of Shipping, 1997) This is widely considered to be a relatively old average age for any fleet.

The communication system in Turkey is a modern and an up-graded system. Although, telephone, fax and computer systems in industrialising cities have been improved, state owned shipping companies (and here, in particular Turkish Maritime Lines), ports and shipyards tend to lack computerised systems. On the contrary, private shipping companies and maritime institutions are facilitated with much more modern equipment.

The general condition of state owned maritime infrastructure in Turkey is fair and needs to be modernised in order to compete with the private sector on both domestic and international platforms. The ports including the major ones which remain state owned, require considerably more modernisation and most of them are not yet computerised (Chamber of Shipping, 1996c). As examples, the Ports of Istanbul, Izmir and Mersin, which are amongst the major ports in Turkey, are also container ports. Although a reasonable range of container handling equipment, i.e. gantry cranes etc exist at these ports, this equipment is not efficiently used largely because of operational deficiencies (Containerisation International, 1995). The technical committee of the Undersecretariat of Shipping in Turkey, has recently inspected the small ports, harbours and quays in the country, in order to assess their needs for a modernisation programme.

The infrastructure feeding the ports from hinterlands in Turkey, for example both the roads and railways, needs to be modernised and improved as a consequence of the increasing demands generated by the local economies in the bigger cities which are exemplified by Istanbul and Izmir, in particular but also a number of other locations.

The traffic through the Straits of Istanbul, connecting the Black Sea and the Sea of Marmara, has been very busy for many years and needs to be controlled closely in order to prevent collisions at sea. As a consequence, sea traffic in the straits of Istanbul will be controlled by electronic equipment installed along the straits in the last few years. These proposed improvements have recently been completed and as such are a substantial improvement upon the technological status of this significant international route (Chamber of Shipping, 1996f).

The ferry ports in Turkey that provide services for operations in the particularly important Italy-Greece-Turkey corridor, are the Ports of Izmir, Cesme, Marmaris and Antalya. These ferry ports and the large majority of the rest of Turkish ferry ports are either operated by Turkish State Railways or the Turkish Maritime Organisation. The characteristics of the locations of the ferry ports of Izmir and Antalya are very similar to each other, whilst the ferry ports of Cesme and Marmaris are also similar to each other. The ferry port of Izmir is situated at the centre of the city and generates a very large volume of traffic. As a consequence, the total area of the ferry quay and passenger terminal are considered to be too small for the current and potential ferry operations. Meanwhile, the port of Antalya has no connections with the railway network. On the other hand, the ferry port of Cesme is situated in a better location compared with the ferry port of Izmir, with a more manageable amount of traffic and wide aprons for cars and passenger. The passenger terminal of the ferry port of Cesme is also too small for the number of potential passengers; however, it is new. The Port of Antalya is also important for seaborne exports.

As a conclusion to the technological context, it is important to highlight that state owned Turkish shipping companies, ports and institutions require some considerable innovation and improvement of their technological facilities in order to compete in the free market conditions that exist. In particular, the major ferry operator, Turkish Maritime Lines requires considerable further investment and to be facilitated with more advanced and modernised computer systems and equipment. On the contrary, the private side of the industry has access to more advanced and modernised technological facilities and equipment. Turkish ports are highly variable in their facilities but would also benefit from some further investment.

Organisational and managerial context

The organisational and managerial context concerns the relationship between maritime companies such as shipowners, ship operators, shipbuilders, maritime institutions, private and state owned maritime establishments and governmental departments and the internal managerial arrangements of those companies.

Since there is no Ministry of Shipping in Turkey, the Turkish maritime industry was managed and controlled by the Undersecretariat of State Ministry for Shipping until 1996. After the establishment of the new coalition Government in 1996, the Turkish maritime industry has started to be controlled and managed by the Undersecretariat of Shipping directly under the Prime Ministry. Unfortunately, various shipping related state companies, such as Turkish Maritime Lines and Turkish Cargo Lines of the Turkish Maritime Organisation, and Turkish State Railways, amongst others, are controlled by up to ten different ministries. Therefore, a notable lack of communication, difficulties in decision-making and information feedback are the main problems arising from this situation. As a result of these problems, establishment of the Ministry of Shipping has emerged as a key political demand of the Turkish shipping industry.

The Turkish Government has promised the establishment of the Ministry, a request that has also been strongly supported by the Chamber of Shipping. Nevertheless, very little action has been taken since the beginning of the 1990s. Despite all the efforts of the Chamber, the Law on the Organisation and Duties of the Ministry of Shipping was not issued by the Grand National Assembly of Turkey by late 1997 despite expectations to the contrary. However, some progress was recently made and it was eventually issued by the Assembly during 1998 but is still waiting to be approved and signed. Overall, little action has been taken by the Government since the beginning of the 1990s in terms of the establishment of the Ministry and central commitment to this plan must be in question.

The owner of most of the major ports is the state in Turkey. Some of them belong to the Turkish Maritime Organisation and the biggest seven ports are owned and operated by Turkish State Railways - both state companies. However, ship operating companies and maritime organisations in Turkey most commonly belong to the private sector. For instance, amongst 108 ship operators, only five of them are state owned companies, these being the Turkish Maritime Organisation, Turkish Cargo Lines, Turkish Maritime Lines, Petrol Ofisi and the Turkish-Libyan joint Maritime Transport Stock Co. (Fairplay Shipping Directory, 1995). The Turkish Maritime Organisation is the owner of Turkish Cargo Lines and Turkish Maritime Lines as noted earlier. Additionally, amongst 21 shipbuilding companies, only one of them is a state owned company, which is the Turkish Shipbuilding Industry Inc. which operates some four shipyards, and remains still under privatisation action by the state.

There are 14 maritime representative organisations in Turkey and all of them are privately owned. Some examples of these organisations are the Istanbul-Marmara-Aegean-Mediterranean and Black Sea Chamber of Shipping, the Mersin Chamber of Shipping, the Turkish Shipbuilders' Association, the Turkish Shipowners' Association and the Turkish Maritime Education Foundation.

Since most of the shipping companies and organisations in Turkey are privately owned, management tends to be based upon a highly competitive market with the dynamism of a free market. Turkey has been taking steps towards action in privatisation since the beginning of the 1990s. However, the Government has been slowed in taking further and quicker steps because of a series of political and bureaucratic problems. It is accepted by the Turkish shipping community that the industry will benefit from the privatisation of the state owned ship operator and ship owning company, Turkish Cargo Lines and some of the major ports and major shipyards located in Istanbul and Izmir. Turkish Cargo Lines, as one of the major shipping companies, is a much slimmer organisation compared with its situation during the beginning of the 1990s after selling a large number of its older ships. However, many of the currently operated vessels need substantial and expensive refurbishment and modernisation. This state owned company cannot contribute to the economy of the country given this current situation.

The managerial organisation of the state owned maritime companies suffer from heavy bureaucracy and decision-making rests with the top management and contrasts markedly with that of the traditional private shipping family companies. In the latter, decision-making and responsibility are commonly shared amongst top management, company staff and workers particularly in those private shipping companies that have been established in more recent years.

It is fairly clear that there is a great difference between the state owned and private maritime establishments in Turkey from an organisational and managerial point of view. The state owned departments and companies reflect the bureaucratic problems mainly caused by shared responsibility and decision-making between different ministries. Therefore, the establishment of a Ministry of Shipping might well help to reduce the organisational and managerial problems that exist. On the contrary, the organisational and managerial characteristics of the private shipping companies match the dynamic free market conditions where a high level of competition takes place. As a consequence, the state owned shipping companies, which are on the government list for privatisation action, exhibit a variety of competition problems in the market that stem from their organisational and managerial inadequacies whilst the private shipping companies actively compete with each other in the dynamic free market; some of them even have foreign joint partners.

Legal context

The first law related to shipping in Turkey was issued in 1864, in effect a translation from the shipping legislation of French Trade Law. However, this initial attempt was substituted by the shipping legislation of German Trade Law in 1929 and was adopted as a part of Turkish Trade Law but specifically applied to the shipping sector (Kalpsuz, 1980). Additionally, other legislation related to ship registration and flags was adopted from German Trade Law dated 1899. The specifically Turkish Trade Law versions of this legislation were updated and revised in 1957, by adopting the new legal output from German Trade Law, that had been updated and revised in 1956 (Kender and Cetingil, 1992).

Sources of Turkish Shipping Law are mainly Turkish Trade Law and various other by-laws, regulations and international agreements. They are outlined below (Kalpsuz, 1980; Kender and Cetingil, 1992; Ministry of Transport, 1992).

Laws

Turkish Trade Law. The main source of Turkish Shipping Law is the 'Shipping' section of Turkish Trade Law. Subsections of this law are related to vessels, operators, captains, passengers, shipping agreements and accidents at sea; the law of cabotage; the law of labour at sea; the law of protection of life and goods at sea; the law of ports; the law of vessels; the law of the coastguard; and the law of the environment.

By-laws

These by-laws constitute the following. The by-law of ship registration issue; the by-law of flagging; the by-law of measuring the tonnages of commercial ships; the by-law of seafarers; the by-law of carrying dangerous goods by commercial ships; and the by-law related to the loading limits of commercial ships.

Regulations

There are a variety of regulations that control the maritime sector. They include those listed below. The Regulation for selling a Turkish commercial ship and for purchasing a new one; the Regulation for subsidies for Turkish shipping and shipbuilding; the Regulation for pilotage; and the Regulation for trade on coasts and borders.

International Agreement

These include the Brussels Agreement dated 1910 and revised in 1967, related to life saving at sea; the Brussels Agreement dated 1924, related to bills of lading and substituted by the Hamburg Regulations dated 1978; the London Protocol dated 1984, related to losses due to fuel pollution at sea; the London Agreement for safety of life at sea (SOLAS) dated 1974 which Turkey decided to adopt only in 1980; the Agreement of London International Loading Limits dated 1966; the International Agreement for Prevention of Marine Pollution (MARPOL) dated 1973 which Turkey formally approved in 1990; the Athens Agreement dated 1974, related to carrying passengers and luggage by sea transport; the International Agreement for training, certificating and standards of shifts for seafarers (STCW), dated 1978 which Turkey signed in 1989; and the Agreement for International Marine Communication via Satellites (INMARSAT) dated 1978 which Turkey signed in 1989.

It is particularly interesting to note that there have been a number of laws, by-laws, regulations and agreements in Turkish Maritime Law that can be considered to be both directly and indirectly related specifically to liner ferry operations which has been one of the most dynamic and volatile of all the shipping sectors in Turkey. Regarding the categories outlined above, Turkish Trade Law, the law of protection of life and goods at sea and the Athens Agreement for carrying passengers and luggage by sea transport are all highly significant and direct pieces of legislation or pseudo-legislation that are directly related to the passenger shipping and ferry sectors. One of the major subsections of Turkish Trade Law is related to the rights of passengers. Details of this subsection consist of rights of passengers to cancel their tickets, their rights in terms of carrying luggage, and their rights to be compensated in the case of various events, such as war, natural disasters etc.

The laws and by-laws that have a rather more indirect relationship in general with ferry operations are listed as follows: the law of transport substructures, the law of development of the shipping fleet and subsidies for shipbuilding facilities, the law relating to subsidies for tourism, the law of the environment, the law of the general status of Turkish State Railways, (which operates and controls the major ports in Turkey), the law of the general status of the Turkish Maritime Organisation, the by-law relating to the subsidy and development policy for Turkish shipping and shipbuilding, the by-law of the application of the law of development of shipping fleets and subsidies for shipbuilding facilities, the by-law relating to maritime transport between Turkey and Italy, and the by-law for the subsidy and development of the Turkish shipping fleet (Ministry of Transport, 1992).

A new regulation known as a 'Line Permit' was issued by the Undersecretariat of Shipping in 1996 aiming to adopt a policy to raise standards of ferry services on international services. This regulation was issued and particularly aimed at the ferry services in the Italy-Greece-Turkey corridor in the Eastern Mediterranean market place as a consequence of various recent problems, including problems stemming from the operation of out-dated ferries and taking advantage of this growing ferry market through the use of unsuitable and at times unsafe vessels.

Stemming from the discussion of this context, it should be noted that there are a number of laws and by-laws both directly and indirectly related to the Turkish maritime industry. However, there remains in Turkey a view that that this body of legislation is too general in nature and lacks sufficient detail. New legislation may be required to be issued as the maritime industry in Turkey continues to increase in economic significance through and beyond the 1990s.

Marketing context

The marketing context has been operationalised in an attempt to focus upon the major shipping markets of Turkey and thus to place the other conceptual contexts of the model related to the Turkish shipping industry in perspective. The major types of shipping services in Turkey relate to the bulk shipping sector and mostly tramp services, tanker shipping and OBO shipping. Approximately 60% of the total merchant fleet consists of bulk carriers, 15% consists of tankers and 8% consists of OBOs. In addition, general cargo carriers have also a considerable share - some 14%, in the total merchant fleet. The general character of the Turkish merchant fleet - with its dominance of bulk carriers, general cargo carriers and OBOs and with relatively fewer container ships and ferries and no cruise ships - reflects the developing and industrialising character of Turkey in general. The major shipping markets of Turkey providing tramp services through bulk carriers are the Mediterranean and the Black Sea markets. The western European, American and the Far Eastern markets are also shipping markets where shipping services are provided by a limited number of regular lines from Turkey.

Although only 1.4% of the Turkish merchant fleet consists of ferries and ro-ro ships, ferry services in the Eastern Mediterranean area and the Italy-Greece-Turkey corridor in particular, is another considerable shipping market of Turkey, which has increased in importance as a consequence of the civil war in the former Yugoslavia, at the beginning of the 1990s. It also provides both an interesting and a detailed case study for the marketing context in Turkish shipping.

As we noted earlier, Turkish people living in Middle and Western Europe, who travelled previously to and from Turkey by road have had to change transport mode to either air or sea transport because of the problems of trying to use road transport throughout the former Yugoslavia. As a result, a dramatic increase in the traffic volume of sea transport in this corridor has been recorded in recent years (Cruise and Ferry Info., 1994) as travellers attempt to by-pass the conflict that continues in this country (LSM, 1994).

The recent considerable ferry traffic growth has been particularly in the total number of passengers carried by the Turkish national ferry operator, Turkish Maritime Lines after 1992 (Turkish Maritime Organisation, 1995). The majority of the passengers in this market place have been the 2.5 million Turkish people living in a variety of European countries (Ministry of Labour and Social Security, 1996) and visiting their families and relatives in Turkey most commonly, but not exclusively, during the summer period (European Commission, 1996).

There were nine ferry operators operating in this corridor in 1994 and the major ferry operator for many years has been Turkish Maritime Lines, as we noted earlier. Some 70% of the entire body of tickets of the passengers of Turkish Maritime Lines in 1994 and 74% of the same in 1995 were sold by the main agency of Turkish Maritime Lines, Reca Agency in Germany (Turkish Maritime Lines, 1995) reflecting both the existing and potential Turkish market in many European countries. Other agency outlets are located in the United Kingdom, Italy, the Netherlands, Austria, Belgium, France, Greece and Northern Cyprus.

Greek ferry operators started to operate between Italy and Turkey via Greece in this corridor during 1991 and in doing so they have been the major companies competing with the Turkish ferry operators. This competition is evidenced by a number of advertising campaigns by Greek operators in Turkish newspapers with the following advertisement logos:

Marlines - 'Turkish cook, Turkish food and Turkish personnel';
Minoan Lines - 'Travel and relax with Minoan Lines';
European Seaways - 'From Italy to Cesme within 32 hours';
Horizon Sea Lines - 'In 48 hours to Cesme';
Medlink Lines - 'Turkish food, Turkish personnel and a place for Islamic praying';
Neta Lines - 'Turkish food, Turkish personnel and traditional Turkish music'.

Each is clearly acknowledging the sizeable Turkish market in this corridor and playing on the demand for services orientated towards this sector.

Unfortunately, various problems exist with the ferry services in this corridor reflecting a failure to appreciate fully the needs of the market and a severe shortage of administrative and economic discipline. These problems include double booking; selling more tickets for cabins than the capacity of the ship allows; limited meal provision; and the sale of tickets through agencies in Germany one year prior to the ferry service date, but receiving no service because of the bankruptcy of seven Turkish operators. In the latter case, no compensation has been paid (Turkish Maritime Lines, 1995). In addition, there is only a limited number of Turkish ferries which are insufficient for the potential Turkish passenger market who have a high preference for Turkish operators and flagged vessels. These are not considered as important problems by some of the ferry operators, but passengers frequently complain about the quality of services after spending between 40-60 hours on board.

As noted earlier, the Undersecretariat for Shipping in Turkey issued a 'Line Permit' regulation for Port State Control and quality standardisation of international ferry services to and from Turkish ports in January 1996 (Undersecretariat of Shipping, 1996). Following from this, Line Permits have not been issued by the Undersecretariat for various ferry operators because they do not match the requirements that are in place. Furthermore, the agencies were also informed by the Undersecretariat of Shipping about the requirements of the ISM Code which have had to be applied to all ferry services operating to and from all European Union ports (including those in Italy and Greece) by the 1st July, 1996.

The ferry market in the Eastern Mediterranean has been a rapidly developing market both from the demand and supply sides and as such it provides an interesting case study of Turkish market developments. As a consequence of the increasing demand for ferry services in this market place, and in the Italy-Greece-Turkey corridor in particular, various operational and economic problems have started to appear. However, it is encouraging to note that the Undersecretariat of Shipping in Turkey has taken a number of immediate actions to resolve these problems and to improve the ferry services within the region.

Logistical context

All modes of transport - land, sea, air, rail and pipeline - are used in Turkey for a variety of different commodities. The majority of transport activity in Turkey is conducted by land transport because the country is situated on a wide land mass of approximately 775,000 square kilometres. However, the mountainous areas in the central, eastern and south-eastern regions of the country create some serious difficulties for investment in tunnels and other earthworks for both roads and railways. The Turkish truck fleet is one of the largest in Europe and is widely used for the physical distribution of goods. The motorway network system has not yet been completed throughout the country. The biggest two cities - Istanbul and Ankara - are connected to each other by a motorway. Orbitals for these metropolitan cities together with the ones for Izmir in the west and Adana in the south are under construction with some parts already being used.

The construction of a railway network commenced during the beginning of this century and has been rapidly widened to give access to large parts of the country. However, railways could not develop in all regions because of the high investment costs and mountainous and geographic structure of this sizeable country. Although there is a railway network with connections from the European network in the northwest and to Iran in the east of the country, railway transport quality is poor and requires considerable technological improvement. However, some railways are important in connecting the major ports to their hinterlands.

Inland water transport is limited compared with that in many west European countries. The main reason for the undeveloped character of inland waterway transport in Turkey stems from the variable flow capacity of rivers, which makes transport difficult particularly during warmer seasons. Inland water transport is currently used to a very limited extent in the Black Sea region in the north of Turkey.

Approximately 90% of the foreign trade of Turkey is carried by seaborne transport. The major ports that are used for intermodal transport are the Ports of Izmir in the west, Istanbul in the northwest and Mersin in the south of the country. Most of the secondary ports as well as these major ports are linked by roads to main highways and airports, and by railways to their hinterlands. Although these major ports are busy with seaborne foreign trade, they tend not to be that busy with cabotage shipping. There are a number container liner shipping services from the Ports of Istanbul and Izmir to western Europe, America and the Far East and the situation, structure and facilities of these ports are suitable for door-to-door intermodal transport. However, the majority of shipping services focus upon the Mediterranean and Black Sea regions. Passenger transport by ferries has been developing in the Mediterranean market after the collapse of the former Yugoslavia. Meanwhile, ro-ro services have also been rapidly developing both in the Mediterranean market between the Ports of Trieste and Venice in Italy and the Ports of Istanbul and Izmir in Turkey and in the Black Sea market between the Port of Constantza in Romania and the Port of Istanbul in Turkey.

Air transport is a rapidly developing transport mode in Turkey with considerable increases during high seasons both in domestic and international lines. There are regular services on international lines to many countries in the world by aircraft under Turkish flag. The state owned and operated airline - Turkish Airlines - is one of the fastest developing and most improved young fleets in the world. The busiest airports are situated close to the biggest cities in Turkey - Istanbul, Ankara and Izmir. In addition, heavy traffic takes place at the airports of Dalaman and Antalya during high seasons.

Pipeline transport is used in Turkey to transport oil from Iraq to the Port of Mersin in the Mediterranean region for distribution to other places by seaborne transport. However, the flow of oil was suspended during the Gulf War which as a consequence, brought heavy losses for the Turkish economy. A recent policy has been developed to prepare tenders for carrying oil between the north-east and south regions of Turkey, which includes the construction of a similar pipeline between Baku in Azerbaijan and Ceyhan in the Mediterranean region in Turkey for onward transport across the Mediterranean Sea.

As a result, all modes of transport are used in Turkey and much of this transport activity stems from the country's geographical and strategic situation between the continents of Europe and Asia. The development of further intermodal transport services for the distribution of goods will undoubtedly continue to occur with the continuing dynamism of the region.

Environmental context

Turkey is a peninsula with a total coast line of approximately 8,000 kilometres. Although the country is surrounded by sea on three sides, this facility is not used efficiently particularly in terms of environmental protection with insufficient attention given to the maritime context. Moreover, there has been a substantial level of unconscious pollution and deformation of natural environment in many places caused by either increasing industrialisation or other related elements.

Sea water tends to be polluted by wastes from land, air or from other seas. The percentages of each type of marine pollution in the region are estimated to be some 44% from the land, 33% airborne wastes, 12% seaborne pollution and wastes from maritime transport, 10% pollution and wastes from off-shore platforms and 1% from other sources. Marine pollution as a result of wastes from maritime transport forms a considerable percentage in the total amount of pollution with oil leakages and ballast water constituting the largest part. These wastes can be grouped under ballast operations, tank cleaning operations, bunker operations, ballast waters, mud with oil particulates, dry waste from vessels, dirty liquid discharges from vessels and from the results of tanker collisions. In addition, the operation of a ship's main and auxiliary engines also causes marine pollution which arises from bunker and engine separation. The percentages of general items causing seaborne marine pollution are ballast water 44%, tanker operations 28%, collisions 22%, off-shore terminals and platforms 5% and maintenance pools 1% (Denizati, 1997).

Another type of marine pollution is created by an increasing imbalanced ecology, which is caused by loading ballast waters into vessels and discharging them into the seas in the other parts of the world. An example of this has taken place recently along the coasts and seas of Turkey with some naturally deep water plants, which did not exist previously in the region and which were carried in ship ballast waters from other seas.

In addition to increasing the level of imbalanced ecology in the seas from ballast waters, oxygen in the water is also destroyed by ballast water that is carrying oil particulates. Moreover, tanker collisions are another cause of marine pollution resulting in the detrimental impacts of the spilt oil upon oxygen levels. The majority of tanker collisions occur in Turkish waters along the straits of Istanbul to the northwest of the country, where substantial dangerous and heavy tanker traffic takes place at present. Therefore, a related shipping policy has been adopted in Turkey to bring some regulations for the improvement of tanker traffic and to avoid such collisions in the straits.

Sea transport is one of the important sources of marine pollutants as noted earlier. Therefore, regulations both improving environmental protection and avoiding marine pollution e.g. IMO regulations, MARPOL etc. have been adopted by the central Government in Turkey. MARPOL 73/78 regulations were adopted by Turkey in 1990. This means that there should be waste water discharge facilities at ports, waste destroying equipment and ballast water separators on board ships and a series of regulated tanker operations which operate according to the protocol signed.

As a result of the recognition of the growing problems of maritime pollution, an environmental association - the Turkish Marine Environmental Protection Association (Turmepa) - was established in 1994 to promote public awareness of marine pollution and to bring forward solutions to the problems of marine pollution in Turkey. Some objectives of the association for 1998 have included forming courses for environmental teachers and writing a guide teacher's textbook, distributing bulletins, posters and brochures, writing introductory books for children, helping to improve the activities of sea scouts, promotional contests, forming information centres and web pages on the internet and promoting projects involved in marine sweepers, marine pollution maps, raising new funds, certificate training programmes and nationwide environmental training centres (Borovali, 1997).

A technical monitoring group was recently established to follow and detect the vessels discharging ballast waters in the Bay of Izmir in the Aegean Sea to the west of Turkey, where a high level of marine pollution takes place caused by sewage flowing directly into the bay. Each ship engine's use of differing amounts of bunker fuel and discharge of differing chemical solutions into the sea is considered a fingerprint of each respective vessel in terms of marine pollution and has provided an effective way of monitoring vessels causing marine pollution.

Although a number of issues that are related to marine protection exist as objectives of the Ministry of Environment in Turkey, they tend not to be used effectively because of the lack of coordination between the ministries and undersecretaries. Environmental issues are thus noted and highlighted by the Undersecretariat of Shipping in an attempt to redress this situation. As we have noted earlier, establishment of a Ministry of Shipping is currently on the agenda of the Turkish Government. Meanwhile, the environmental objectives of the Ministry, which were recently noted in general items by the Undersecretariat of Shipping can be summarised as follows:

Establishment of a Port Authority system for marine and environmental protection in the Black Sea and the

Mediterranean Sea on the north and south coasts of Turkey.
Establishment of ballast water treatment plants on the coasts of Turkey.
Signing national and international agreements related to marine and environmental protection and improving personal and technological substructures.
Developing a law against oil pollution.
Effective use of protocols signed previously for the protection of the Black Sea and the Mediterranean Sea, in particular.
(Undersecretariat of Shipping, 1997).

A number of issues related to marine pollution were listed within the law for the establishment of the Ministry of Shipping, which include in particular, the implementation of a legal action against ship collisions causing marine pollution and provision and monitoring of new issues for the environmental protection of the seas against marine pollutants (Ministry of State, 1997).

A considerable number of issues exist on the list of important items of different ministry agendas and a number of these issues are beginning to be implemented and some monitored by a range of authorities in Turkey. Some importance is now being given to environmental protection and the other aspects of marine pollution; however, additional importance is going to be needed to achieve more effective processes and a greater guarantee of efficient results.

Some conclusions to the conceptual contexts

A conceptual model has been developed and a number of conceptual contexts operationalised for the Turkish maritime industry. Differing contexts can be considered more or less important each having both direct and indirect effects upon the shipping and ports industries. The more significant issues centre around the geopolitical situation within Turkey and its effects upon the structure and policies of government, the liberalisation policy adopted for the economy from the beginning of the 1980s and its effects upon the levels, direction and characteristics of the import and export trades, the impact of these factors upon the social life of the Turkish people and the knock-on effects for prices, wages, education and seafarer training and expectations, increasing migration from the rural to the urban areas, and therefore the increasing rate of unemployment together with persistently high inflation rates, direct privatisation policies for a large number of the shipping institutions such as ports and shipyards, the functions and status of the sizeable bulk shipping sector in Turkey, and need for further legislation related in particular to passenger shipping. In addition, the role and activities of Turkish society in various western European countries presents an interesting case study of a number of issues affecting the maritime sector, and in particular its impact upon the rapidly developing Eastern Mediterranean ferry market, providing the major link between these communities and Turkey itself. In addition, logistical and environmental issues are also important because of their crucial and direct impact upon the Turkish shipping and ports industry. Consequently, these contexts provide an essential general background for any analysis of the Turkish maritime industry that is to take place in the forthcoming chapters.

3. Liberalisation policy and Turkish shipping after the 1980s

Introduction

This section of the book presents a discussion of recent developments in the Turkish maritime sector following the liberalisation policy introduced from the early 1980s. Liberalisation in the Turkish economy was promoted during the Prime Ministry of Mr Ozal in the beginning of the 1980s as we noted earlier in the section that discussed the economic context of the conceptual model of Turkish shipping. As a result of this outward looking policy, new strategies were developed for the Turkish economy which had a major impact for the maritime sector.

The liberalisation policies of the Turkish economy have had both positive and negative effects as we also noted earlier within the economic context. The programmes adopted within this policy have not yet been successful in achieving the objectives set for the long term. A major reason for this was explained earlier and stemmed from the liberalisation and stabilisation programmes which were adopted simultaneously, instead of stabilising the economy first before undertaking a programme of liberalisation. However, although there is instability and uncertainty both in the economic and political situation in Turkey, this liberalisation policy still has had some positive effects upon the economy in the transition period, up until the present time (1998).

The economic liberalisation policy has tended to encourage a free market model to be adopted for Turkey. Inevitably, increase in foreign trade activity as a consequence of this action has had direct impacts upon the shipping industry with approximately 90% of Turkish foreign trade depending upon maritime transport. The shipping industry has also been more generally affected by the liberalisation policy as have many other industries in Turkey. As a result, the Turkish shipping industry has registered a significant increase in both activity and development since the mid 1980s and the beginning of the 1990s in particular.

The Turkish merchant fleet

The Turkish shipping industry is outlined in this section in an attempt to give a broad picture of its significance both domestically and within the world. This industry has continued to show consistent growth since the middle of the 1980s reflecting the dynamics of the free market conditions provided by the liberalisation policy of the Turkish economy. The industry preserves its position as one of the leading industries in the country.

The size of the Turkish shipping fleet is continuing to grow with an increasing trend as the Turkish economy further liberalises and therefore, Turkish shipowners gain greater access to funding enabling the fleet to be modernised. Turkish ship operations transformed dramatically the operation of 300-400 dwt of vessels in the 1940s to a fleet reaching a total of 1.5 million dwt in 1980 and 2 million dwt in 1982 with the support of Government subsidies, the Chamber of Shipping and the Association of Shipowners (LSM, 1993). During the Prime Ministry of Mr Ozal at the beginning of the 1980s and with an increase in economic liberalisation policies, the self reliance of Turkey increased and the doors of the country were opened wide. In parallel to this, international trade and relations increased and the shipping industry has consequently grown stronger.

The size of the Turkish merchant fleet nearly tripled in three years and reached 5.81 million dwt in 1985 and then nearly doubled in five years by reaching 10.31 million dwt by the end of 1995. This size reached 10.89 million dwt with 1179 vessels by the end of 1996 (Chamber of Shipping, 1996f); however, a decrease of 3% in the total tonnage to 10.56 million dwt with 1197 vessels by the end of 1997 was then registered (Chamber of Shipping, 1998a). Whilst the number of newly built vessels has shown a slight increase, the recent decrease in the total tonnage of the fleet is mainly a result of the decrease in the purchase of vessels from other countries. The annual growth of the total fleet together with the annual distribution between 1987 and 1997 of the Turkish merchant fleet by vessel types and total number of

50

vessels are listed in Tables 7 and 8. Major vessel types in the merchant fleet are general cargo, bulk carrier, container and OBO vessels, oil tankers, ro-ro vessels and ferries. The remaining vessels, which are grouped as other vessels, are listed as chemical tankers, LPG tankers, asphalt tankers, tugs and intracity passenger vessels and ferries.

The Turkish fleet constituted approximately 8 million dwt of approximately 1000 vessels with an average age of more than 20 years, in 1993 (Fairplay, 1993). The dominant sector has been bulk carriers accounting for 60% of the fleet in dwt at present (1998).

Table 7
Annual growth of the Turkish merchant fleet and distribution of vessels between 1987 and 1997 (million dwt)

Vessel type	1987	1988	1989	1990	1991	1992	1993	1994	1995	1996	1997
Bulk carrier	1.84	1.74	1.79	2.27	2.40	2.72	3.84	4.27	5.76	6.44	6.85
General cargo	1.39	1.39	1.34	1.34	1.37	1.34	1.40	1.47	1.46	1.47	1.42
Tanker	1.38	1.38	1.53	1.56	1.56	1.78	2.08	1.67	1.70	1.61	0.95
OBO	0.52	0.29	0.38	0.38	0.53	0.53	0.80	0.96	1.04	0.92	0.82
Ro-ro & Ferry	0.02	0.03	0.03	0.02	0.03	0.04	0.03	0.09	0.14	0.15	0.17
Container	0.01	0.01	0.01	0	0	0	0	0.01	0.02	0.05	0.09
Others	0.08	0.07	0.09	0.07	0.08	0.09	0.11	1.03	0.19	0.25	0.26
Total	**5.24**	**4.91**	**5.17**	**5.64**	**5.97**	**6.50**	**8.26**	**9.50**	**10.31**	**10.89**	**10.56**

Sources: Chamber of Shipping (1996c), (1997), (1998a).

The Turkish merchant fleet consists mainly of handysize and panamax bulkers and also some 45,000 dwt bulkers the majority of which are Turkish flagged. Most of the handysize vessels are owned by interests in Istanbul, Turkey's commercial heart, and are cross trading in a competitive market in the Black Sea to Bulgarian, Ukranian and Russian ports.

The average age of the Turkish merchant fleet had fallen to approximately 18.4 years in 1995 but rose again to 19 years in 1996, which was more than the average age of the world fleet; it has again recently declined marginally to

17 years (Chamber of Shipping, 1997). The distribution of the Turkish merchant fleet by age groups and tonnage at the ends of 1995, 1996 and 1997 are listed in Tables 9, 10 and 11. The percentages of the age groups for the total tonnages are also illustrated in the same tables.

Table 8
Annual growth of the Turkish merchant fleet and distribution of vessels in terms of total numbers between 1987 and 1997

Vessel type	1987	1988	1989	1990	1991	1992	1993	1994	1995	1996	1997
Bulk carrier	54	51	50	65	70	70	109	121	157	173	181
General cargo	454	457	452	454	453	460	472	479	476	475	469
Tanker	79	81	85	90	90	101	102	100	99	103	98
OBO	5	3	4	4	5	5	7	8	9	8	7
Ro-ro & Ferry	16	17	17	16	18	19	21	28	37	40	42
Container	1	1	1	0	0	0	0	1	3	7	11
Others	212	220	230	239	263	299	301	313	362	373	389
Total	**821**	**830**	**839**	**868**	**899**	**954**	**1012**	**1050**	**1143**	**1179**	**1197**

Sources: Chamber of Shipping (1996c), (1997), (1998a).

Table 9
Age groups of the Turkish merchant fleet (31.12.1995)

Age group	Number of vessels	Tonnage (million dwt)	% of total tonnage
0-4	81	0.18	1.8
5-9	127	0.33	3.2
10-14	193	2.19	21.2
15-19	199	2.61	25.3
20-24	204	3.72	36.1
25-29	146	1.03	10.0
over 30	192	0.25	2.4
TOTAL	**1142**	**10.31**	**100**

Source: Chamber of Shipping (1996c).

Table 10
Age groups of the Turkish merchant fleet (31.12.1996)

Age group	Number of vessels	% in the total number of vessels	Tonnage (million dwt)	% of total tonnage
0-4	81	6.9	0.21	1.9
5-9	119	10.1	0.31	2.8
10-14	197	16.7	2.14	19.7
15-19	180	15.3	2.35	21.6
20-24	244	20.7	4.40	40.4
25-29	148	12.5	1.20	11.0
over 30	210	17.8	0.28	2.6
TOTAL	**1179**	**100**	**10.89**	**100**

Source: Chamber of Shipping (1997).

Table 11
Age groups of the Turkish merchant fleet (31.12.1997)

Age group	Number of vessels	% of total vessel number	Tonnage (million dwt)	% of total tonnage
0-4	80	6.7	0.35	3.3
5-9	115	9.6	0.39	3.7
10-14	190	15.9	2.03	19.2
15-19	191	16.0	2.08	19.7
20-24	235	19.6	3.76	35.6
25-29	151	12.6	1.60	15.2
over 30	235	19.6	0.35	3.3
TOTAL	**1197**	**100**	**10.56**	**100**

Source: Chamber of Shipping (1998a).

Table 12
Age groups of the Turkish merchant fleet in terms of vessel types (31.12.1997)

Vessel type	Age groups				
	0-4	5-9	10-19	over 20	Total
General cargo	43	30	185	211	469
Bulk carrier	---	5	112	64	181
Tanker	3	6	26	63	98
Ro-Ro & Ferry	4	7	8	23	42
Container	11	---	---	---	11
Others	19	67	47	256	389
TOTAL	**80**	**115**	**381**	**621**	**1197**

Source: Chamber of Shipping (1998a).

The majority of vessels lie between the ages of 10 and 24 years and this is reflected in the tables; more specifically 52% of the merchant fleet in terms of total numbers and 75% in terms of total tonnages lie between the ages of 10 and 24 years in 1997. Similarly, 53% of the total vessels in the fleet and 82% of the total tonnage were between the ages 10 and 24 years in 1996. In addition, Table 12 illustrates distribution of vessel ages in terms of vessel types in 1997. As also illustrated in the table, the majority of vessel types are more than 10 years of age with the exception of container vessels, which are all younger than four years.The most recent data related to the total capacity of the Turkish merchant fleet is a total tonnage of 10.42 million dwt with 1,200 vessels at the end of the first quarter in 1998 (Forum, 1998). Details of the fleet at that time are illustrated in Table 13. As is illustrated in Tables 7, 8 and 13, no changes have taken place with regards to bulk carriers, ro-ro vessels and ferries. On the contrary, there are some slight changes in general cargo, container, OBO vessels and tankers with the addition of one container vessel, one general cargo carrier and one tanker to the merchant fleet and the decline of the OBOs by one vessel. Seven hundred and eighteen of the vessels were built in national shipyards whilst 482 of them were imported either as second-hand vessels or newly built in foreign shipyards.

The Turkish merchant fleet in the world

The total merchant fleet in the world was 681.800 million dwt with a total of 36,250 vessels by the end of 1994 and was 702.343 million dwt with a total 37,015 vessels by the end of 1995 (ISL, 1995; ISL, 1996). Panama, Liberia and Greece dominated the figures and were ranked in the first three places in the world merchant fleet both in 1994 and 1995.

The Turkish merchant fleet was placed 23rd in the world merchant fleet in 1992 (ISL, 1993). It was placed 19th in 1993 (ISL, 1994) and 17th in 1994 (ISL, 1995) with a share of 1.4% in the world merchant fleet with a total of 9.50 million dwt by the end of 1994. This share was 1.5% with a total of 10.31 million dwt by the end of 1995 (Chamber of Shipping, 1995a; Chamber of Shipping, 1996a) and the Turkish merchant fleet was 16th in the world in 1995 (ISL, 1996) as illustrated in Table 14. In addition, it was again placed 16th at the end of 1996 with a total of 10.89 million dwt as illustrated in Table 15 and a share of 1.5% of the world merchant fleet (Chamber of Shipping, 1997; Undersecretariat of Shipping, 1997). Similarly, the Turkish merchant fleet was placed 17th at the end of 1997 sharing 1.4% of the world merchant fleet in terms of total tonnage (Chamber of Shipping, 1998a) as illustrated in Table 16.

Table 13
Turkish merchant fleet in terms of vessel types under Turkish flag (31.03.1998)

Vessel type	Total number	Total tonnage (million dwt)	% in the total tonnage
Bulk carrier	181	6.85	65.8
General cargo	470	1.42	13.6
Tanker	99	0.95	9.1
OBO	6	0.66	6.3
Ro-Ro & Ferry	42	0.17	1.6
Container	12	0.11	1.1
Others	390	0.26	2.5
TOTAL	1,200	10.42	100

Source: Forum (1998).

The Turkish merchant fleet has been a growing merchant fleet in general terms for some time, reflecting the characteristics of a developing country with the majority of the merchant fleet focussing upon bulk and general cargo carriers with the minority in container vessels, passenger vessels and ferries. In other words, the Turkish merchant fleet mostly consists of bulk carriers, general cargo carriers, tankers and OBOs, which are mostly used for tramp shipping in Turkish seaborne foreign trade and the cross trades (see Table 7). The percentages of the distribution of the Turkish merchant fleet by vessel types and their percentages in the world merchant fleet are also illustrated in Table 17.

Freight rates in Turkey tend to be lower than the ones in developed countries because the majority of cargoes consist of dry bulk as noted earlier and the type of carriage is mostly tramp shipping (Chamber of Shipping, 1997) characterised by small and medium size companies. On the contrary, maritime companies of a larger size have been operating as liner traders using more sophisticated, more modern and larger vessels. The regular lines are concentrated within the European continent, in the Mediterranean and the Black Sea. Furthermore, the majority of shipowners in Turkey are also ship operators and shippers and as a consequence, it cannot be assumed that freight rates tend to favour either shippers or shipowners.

In addition to the world merchant fleet, Table 18 also illustrates the merchant fleets of Turkey in comparison with those of its neighbouring countries with which it has its closest economic relations.

Seaborne foreign trade

Turkish foreign trade increased from 47.1 million tons in 1985 to 85.5 million tons in 1994. The total value of Turkish foreign trade doubled from 21.3 billion US dollars in 1985 to 41.4 billion US dollars in 1994 (Union of Turkish Chambers, 1994). In addition, it increased by approximately 50% between 1994 and 1997. The annual growth of Turkish foreign trade, between 1985 and 1997 is listed in Table 19.

The total amount of goods carried by maritime transport as foreign trade in Turkey was 41.17 million tons in 1985 with 11.46 million tons of exports and 29.71 million tons of imports. The total amount of goods carried by maritime transport reached 82.98 million tons in 1993, but dropped to 74.74 million tons in 1994 (Chamber of Shipping, 1995a). This amount increased again to reach 84.18 million tons in 1995 (Chamber of Shipping, 1996d) and 112.37 million tons in 1997 (SIS, 1998). The development of sea transport in Turkey between 1985 and 1997 is listed in Table 20. The total amount of goods carried by vessels under Turkish and foreign flags is also listed in Table 20. It is clear from the same table and from Figures 2 and 3 that approximately 90% of Turkish foreign trade is carried by sea transport.

The total of exports in Turkish foreign trade carried by vessels with Turkish and foreign flags is listed in Table 21. The total amount of export goods carried by Turkish flag vessels was 2.45 million tons in 1985 and reached 7.96 million tons in 1995 but dropped slightly to 7.44 million tons in 1996. In addition, total imports in Turkish foreign trade carried by vessels with Turkish and foreign flags are listed in Table 22. The total amount of import goods carried by Turkish and foreign flag vessels was 15.83 million tons in 1985 and reached 27.20 million tons in 1995 and 28.20 million tons in 1996.

It is also clear from Tables 20 to 22 that the total amount of foreign trade cargo carried by vessels under the Turkish flag continues to decline year by year, which as a consequence causes an increase in the total freight payment for vessels under foreign flags. The total amount of freight income received from the carriage of cargoes by Turkish flag vessels between 1985 and 1989 was approximately US$ 3.2 billion. However, the total amount of freight rates paid for carriage of cargoes by foreign flag vessels during the same period amounted to approximately US$ 5 billion.

Table 14
The world merchant fleet (31.12.1995)

Country	Total tonnage (million dwt)	Total % in the world merchant fleet
1. Panama	107.538	15.3
2. Liberia	96.034	13.7
3. Greece	51.439	7.3
4. Cyprus	39.256	5.6
5. The Bahamas	35.407	5.0
6. Norway	32.423	4.6
7. Malta	28.561	4.1
8. Japan	27.200	3.9
9. China	23.700	3.4
10. Singapore	20.082	2.9
11. Hong Kong	15.125	2.2
12. U.S.A.	14.775	2.1
13. Philippines	13.603	1.9
14. Russia	12.968	1.8
15. India	11.120	1.6
16. Turkey	**10.310**	**1.5**
17. Korea	9.874	1.4
18. Taiwan	9.136	1.3
19. St.Vincent	8.506	1.2
20. Italy	8.319	1.2
21. Brazil	8.022	1.1
22. Denmark	7.487	1.1
23. U.K.	7.273	1.0
24. Germany	6.368	0.9
25. France	5.863	0.8
26. Marshall Islands	5.134	0.7
27. Ukraine	4.865	0/7
28. The Bermudas	4.790	0.7
29. The Netherlands	4.724	0.7
30. Others	72.184	10.3
TOTAL	**702.343**	**100**

Source: ISL (1996).

Table 15
Top countries in the world merchant fleet (31.12.1996)

Country	Total tonnage (million dwt)	Total number of vessels
1. Panama	120.9	4579
2. Liberia	94.8	1574
3. Greece	47.5	1308
4. The Bahamas	37.0	1031
5. Cyprus	36.7	1552
6. Norway	32.8	1138
7. Malta	31.6	1171
8. Singapore	25.7	875
9. Japan	25.7	3351
10. China	23.7	2061
11. Hong Kong	13.7	304
12. Philippines	13.6	907
13. U.S.A.	13.4	.380
14. Russia	11.2	1874
15. India	10.9	392
16. Turkey	**10.89**	**1179**
17. Korea	10.5	722
18. St.Vincent	9.7	793
19. Taiwan	9.2	238
20. U.K.	8.1	447
21. Marshall Islands	7.9	112
22. Italy	7.9	647
23. Denmark	7.6	513

Source: ISL (1997).

Table 16
Top countries in the world merchant fleet (31.12.1997)

Country	Total tonnage (million dwt)	Total % in the world merchant fleet (tonnage)	Total vessels
1. Panama	136.1	18.3	4834
2. Liberia	95.7	12.9	1599
3. Greece	43.1	5.8	1199
4. The Bahamas	38.3	5.2	1070
5. Malta	37.5	5.0	1312
6. Cyprus	36.1	4.9	1533
7. Norway	33.9	4.6	1170
8. Singapore	29.0	3.9	968
9. Japan	24.4	3.3	3510
10. China	22.4	3.0	2045
11. Philippines	13.3	1.8	935
12. U.S.A.	12.9	1.7	375
13. India	11.0	1.5	390
14. St.Vincent	11.0	1.5	885
15. Marshall Islands	10.7	1.4	129
16. Korea	10.6	1.4	742
17. Turkey	**10.6**	**1.4**	**1197**
18. U.K.	9.9	1.3	460
19. Russia	9.6	1.3	1755
20. Hong Kong	9.5	1.3	268
21. Taiwan	8.9	1.2	232
22. Germany	7.9	1.1	631
23. The Bermudas	7.3	1.0	1125
24. Others	113.9	15.2	10136
TOTAL	**743.6**	**100**	**38,500**

Source: Chamber of Shipping (1998a).

Table 17
The Turkish merchant fleet in the world (31.12.1997)

Vessel type	Total no.	Total tonnage in 1997 (million dwt)	% in the Turkish merchant fleet (by total tonnage)	% in that class of the world merchant fleet (by total tonnage)	% in the world merchant fleet (by total tonnage)
Bulk carrier	181	6.85	65	2.7	0.9
General cargo	469	1.42	13	1.9	0.2
Tanker	98	0.95	9	0.3	0.1
OBO	7	0.82	8	4.2	0.1
Others	442	0.52	5	0.5	0.1
TOTAL	**1197**	**10.56**	**100**	---	**1.4**

Sources: ISL (1996); Chamber of Shipping (1997), (1998a).

Table 18
Merchant fleets of Turkey and neighbouring countries (31.12.1996)

Countries	Total tonnage (million dwt)	Annual change (%)
Greece	47.58	-7.5
Cyprus	36.76	-6.4
Russia	11.82	-13.0
Turkey	**10.89**	**+2.2**
Iran	6.15	+33.6
Romania	3.44	+0.6
Bulgaria	1.61	-0.8
Iraq	0.78	-41.9

Source: ISL (1997).

Table 19
Annual growth of Turkish foreign trade between 1985-1997

Year	Total amount (million tons)			Total value (billion US$)		
	Export	Import	Total	Export	Import	Total
1985	13.79	33.33	47.12	9.96	11.34	21.30
1986	13.22	35.59	48.81	7.46	11.10	18.56
1987	14.26	45.55	59.81	10.19	14.16	24.35
1988	21.89	46.30	68.19	11.66	14.34	26.00
1989	17.42	47.17	64.59	11.62	15.79	27.41
1990	18.65	50.89	69.54	12.96	22.30	35.26
1991	23.74	47.61	71.35	13.59	21.05	34.64
1992	26.05	50.57	76.62	14.72	22.87	37.59
1993	21.60	65.50	87.10	15.35	29.43	44.78
1994	28.58	56.89	85.47	18.11	23.27	41.38
1995	26.55	67.45	94.00	21.64	35.71	57.35
1996	24.81	77.58	102.39	23.08	42.46	65.54
1997	48.69	76.79	125.48	26.25	48.66	74.91

Sources: Union of Turkish Chambers (1994), Chamber of Shipping (1998a).

Table 23 illustrates the total of Turkish foreign trade shipping according to cargo types by the end of 1997. It is clear from the table that dry bulk, liquid bulk, general cargo, oil and ore are the major cargoes in foreign trades made to and from Turkey. The leading shipping sectors both in exports and imports goods are tanker and OBO shipping followed by general cargo shipping and then, dry bulk shipping. Tanker and OBO shipping have a share of 48% of total foreign trade shipping with general cargo shipping sharing 30% and dry bulk shipping sharing 14% of the same total amount (Chamber of Shipping, 1998a). The major cargoes within general cargo shipping are industrial products and timber whilst cereals, agricultural products and coal are the main cargo types that dominate the dry bulk shipping sector.

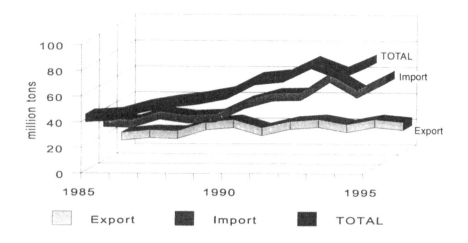

Figure 2
Turkish foreign trade carried by sea transport between 1985 and 1995

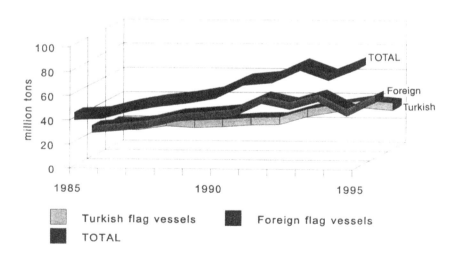

Figure 3
The distribution of Turkish foreign trade carried by Turkish and foreign flag vessels between 1985 and 1995

Table 20
The development of Turkish sea transport between 1985 and 1997 (million tons)

Year	Export	Import	Total	Carriage by Turkish flag vessels	Carriage by foreign flag vessels
1985	11.46	29.71	41.17	18.28	22.89
1986	13.39	29.03	42.42	17.65	24.77
1987	12.94	35.59	48.53	21.02	27.51
1988	19.71	32.81	52.52	19.70	32.82
1989	21.53	33.67	55.20	20.59	34.61
1990	15.24	43.88	59.12	22.31	36.81
1991	20.34	49.89	70.23	22.71	47.52
1992	21.92	50.50	72.42	29.54	42.88
1993	18.10	64.88	82.98	33.49	49.49
1994	22.11	52.63	74.74	36.99	37.75
1995	20.17	64.01	84.18	35.16	49.02
1996	18.85	72.84	91.69	36.06	55.63
1997	37.01	75.36	112.37	32.84	79.53

Sources: Chamber of Shipping (1996a), (1996b), (1996d), (1998a).

Table 21
Total exports carried by Turkish and foreign flag vessels between 1985 and 1996 (million tons)

Year	Export by Turkish flag vessels	Export by foreign flag vessels	Total export
1985	2.45	9.01	11.46
1986	4.66	8.73	13.39
1987	4.36	8.59	12.95
1988	5.02	14.69	19.71
1989	5.23	16.30	21.32
1990	4.72	10.52	15.24
1991	6.03	14.32	20.35
1992	8.29	13.63	21.92
1993	8.63	9.47	18.10
1994	10.50	11.61	22.11
1995	7.96	12.21	20.17
1996	7.44	11.41	18.85

Sources: Chamber of Shipping (1995a), (1996d), (1997).

Table 22
Total imports carried by Turkish and foreign flag vessels between 1985 and 1996 (million tons)

Year	Import by Turkish flag vessels	Import by foreign flag vessels	Total import
1985	15.83	13.88	29.71
1986	13.02	16.01	29.03
1987	16.66	18.93	35.59
1988	14.69	18.12	32.81
1989	15.36	18.31	33.67
1990	17.59	26.29	43.88
1991	16.68	33.21	49.89
1992	21.25	29.25	50.50
1993	24.86	40.02	64.88
1994	26.49	26.14	52.63
1995	27.20	36.81	64.01
1996	28.62	44.22	72.84

Sources: Chamber of Shipping (1995a), (1996d), (1997)

Major sectors in Turkish shipping

The major shipping sectors in terms of cargo types within total foreign trade shipping in Turkey have been traditionally tanker and OBO shipping, general cargo shipping and dry bulk shipping. In addition, liquid bulk shipping also has an important place within the total bulk shipping sector. Container shipping, ro-ro shipping and ferry services have been rapidly developing in Turkey since the beginning of the 1990s and as a result, their significance within the Turkish shipping industry is also discussed briefly in this section in addition to the more expansive explanations of the major shipping areas.

Bulk shipping

Bulk shipping has always been and continues to remain one of the major shipping areas of the overall foreign trade shipping of Turkey. Some 19% of total foreign trade shipping in 1997 was undertaken by the bulk shipping sector, dominated by dry bulk shipping with a 14% share of the total amount. Total tonnages for bulk carriers were 6.85 million dwt for the dry bulk sector with a total of 181 vessels, and 0.16 million dwt for liquid bulk carriers with 46 vessels in the same year (Chamber of Shipping, 1998a). Dry bulk shipping is a dynamic shipping area in the foreign trades of the country and tramp shipping has dominated the trades in this area of the shipping industry. Cereals, agricultural products and coal are the main cargo types of the dry bulk shipping sector in Turkey.

General cargo shipping

General cargo shipping has been the second major shipping area in the foreign trade shipping of Turkey for many years and registered a total share of 30% in the cargo carried in 1997. Industrial products, textile products and timber are major cargo types in this area.

Table 23
Total Turkish foreign trade shipping in terms of cargo types (31.12.1997)

Type of shipping	Total tonnage (million dwt)	Total number of vessels	Total foreign trade shipping Exports (m. tns)	Imports (m. tns)
Dry bulk shipping	6.85	181	1.06	14.45
Liquid bulk shipping	0.16	46	1.11	4.97
General cargo shipping	1.42	469	12.13	21.92
Tanker and OBO	1.77	105	22.01	31.89
(Oil)	(0.95)	(98)	(18.46)	(26.62)
(OBO)	(0.82)	(7)	(3.55)	(5.27)
Others	0.36	396	0.70	2.13
Total	**10.56**	**1197**	**37.01**	**75.36**

Source: Chamber of Shipping (1998a)

Tanker and OBO shipping

Tanker shipping and OBO shipping were another significant area within foreign trade shipping of Turkey in recent years and this trend continued during 1997. 48% of the total foreign trade cargoes carried by sea transport were made by tanker and OBO shipping with the largest proportion of this represented by tanker shipping. Tanker shipping in Turkey has been developing rapidly over the last 10 years. The total amount of exports of oil carried by tankers was only 4.3 million tons in 1987 but had increased to 18.5

million tons in 1997. Similarly, imports of oil carried by tankers was 15.2 million tons in 1987 but had increased by 75% in 1997 to 26.6 million tons in 1997 (Chamber of Shipping, 1998a).

Container shipping

Container shipping in the Turkish maritime industry has been rapidly developing since the beginning of the 1990s in parallel with the rapid development of container shipping within intermodal transport in the world. The Ports of Izmir, Istanbul (Haydarpasa) and Mersin, owned by Turkish State Railways (TSR), have been the most active ports in terms of container traffic. In addition to these ports, container traffic has also increased at some of the private ports such as the Ports of Gemport and Armaport. Container handling has been approximately half or more than half of the total cargo handled at

Table 24
Total containers handled at Ports of Turkish State Railways between 1993 and 1997 (million tons)

Port	1993	1994	1995	1996	1997
Izmir	1.960	2.431	2.767	3.331	3.705
Istanbul	1.855	1.654	2.428	2.953	3.024
Mersin	1.251	1.351	1.607	2.004	2.850
Iskenderun	0.008	0.001	0.007	0.002	0.002
Derince	0.024	0.017	0.036	0.111	0.075
Bandirma	---	---	---	---	---
Samsun	0.031	0.015	0.012	0.020	0.030
Total	**5.129**	**5.469**	**6.857**	**8.421**	**9.686**

Source: Turkish State Railways (1998)

Turkon Line Turkon Line is a company established in 1997 as a part of the Kasif Kalkavan Shipping Group, which is one of the many shipping groups of companies that are owned by the Kalkavan Family. In addition, the Yardimci Shipping Group also has some shares in Turkon Line. The company's shipping interests tend to be focused upon the liner container shipping sector in the Mediterranean, Eastern Mediterranean and American markets aiming to provide a highly competitive freight rate. Turkon Line has brought increased competition into the marketplace and increased the share of vessels under Turkish flags by operating a number of container lines around the world (The World, 1998b). Being the first full container shipping company operating their own newly built container vessels under Turkish flag, it is anticipated that the company will continue to benefit from this arrangement and thus will be able to reduce payments of freight rates to vessels operating under foreign flags. The company owns and operates a fleet of eight full-container vessels which is made up as follows:

M/V Alkin Kalkavan; 1,145 TEU/12,060 dwt; built in 1997.
M/V Besire Kalkavan; 1,145 TEU/12,060 dwt; built in 1997.
M/V Mukaddes Kalkavan; 1,145 TEU/12,060 dwt; built in 1997.
M/V Yardimci; 728 TEU/7,450 dwt; built in 1997.
M/V Cimil; 426 TEU/6,000 dwt; built in 1997.
M/V Aron; 333 TEU/4,856 dwt; built in 1995.
M/V Andon; 343 TEU/4,962 dwt; built in 1994.
M/V Mehmet Kalkavan; 600 TEU/12,232 dwt; built in 1993.

The vessels have been operating on a number of container trading lines (The World, 1998b) of which the line in the Eastern Mediterranean is also known as the "shuttle line" for marketing purposes:

Mediterranean market: Istanbul - Gemlik - Izmir - Valencia - Barcelona - Marseilles - Genoa - Piraeus
Eastern Mediterranean market: Istanbul - Gemlik - Izmir - Piraeus - Mersin - Beirut - Alexandria
American market: Istanbul - Gemlik - Izmir - New York - Norfolk - Charleston - Piraeus.

The company uses the facilities and services of the Ports of Izmir, Istanbul and Armaport. The Port of Istanbul in the near future will be substituted by the Port of Armaport in terms of the provision of services for the Mediterranean and American liner markets. The Kalkavan Shipping Group owns a proportion of the shares of the latter port providing an added incentive for this move. Turkon Line managers have been developing services to operate as a door-to-door multimodal transport company and a regional carrier by also investing in a fleet of 100 trucks and establishing an outlet office in the USA.

Arkas Shipping Group In addition to Turkon Line, Arkas Shipping Group also has a significant place within the container shipping sector of Turkey. Arkas Shipping Group - an Izmir based group of shipping companies - has been operating within the industry since the beginning of the 1980s. The Group is mainly concerned with freight forwarding, logistics, and air cargo transportation along with ship operating activities and owns two container vessels of 580 TEUs each. Arkas Shipping Group obtained a 25% share of the container traffic in Turkey by carrying a total of 248,500 TEUs in 1997 (Cargo News, 1998) operating regular services between the Port of Gioia Tauro in Italy, which is one of the leading hub ports in the Mediterranean region, the Port of Malta and a variety of ports in Turkey, in particular.

Ro-Ro Shipping

Foreign trade by land transport between south-eastern Turkey and the Middle Eastern countries has long been considered important because of its volume and value, totalling an annual contribution of US$ 400 million to the national economy until the 1990s. Unfortunately, the Gulf crisis in the Middle East in the beginning of the 1990s directly cut down foreign trades in the area leading land transporters to look for other markets. In addition, the civil war which started in the former Yugoslavia during those years, directly and negatively affected land transport between Turkey and eastern and south-eastern Europe because of Turkey's relative geographical location to the conflict. Land transport by trucks to this area in Europe was either impossible in some places or very difficult in a number of others. As a result of these difficulties and the need to reach the Central and south-east European countries for foreign trades, ro-ro shipping began to develop rapidly in Turkey. By bringing together the advantages of combined and intermodal transport, frequent and regular services between Turkey and Italy have been developed to by-pass the area of conflict to reach both the Mediterranean and Central European countries.

Although there was a crisis in the Turkish economy in 1994, the shipping industry was not badly affected by the crisis unlike many other industrial sectors. In a similar fashion, ro-ro shipping was in a good economic and financial situation in 1994 and even contributed US$ 0.55 billion to the national economy by carrying 4,235,000 million tons of cargo (The Economist, 1995) with an annual increase of 9% both in the total cargo carried and foreign exchange contribution to the national economy.

The Aegean Ro-Ro Company In addition to the ro-ro shipping services operated by Turkish Cargo Lines and the UND Shipping Group, the Aegean Ro-Ro Company was recently established by one of the leading land transport companies - Esin Intermodal Transport Company - which operates a fleet of 150 trailers in distribution services to and from many European countries. The ro-ro services of this company will constitute three vessels operating between Trieste in Italy and the Port of Tekirdag in the Marmara region in the north-west of Turkey commencing in late 1998 (International Transport News, 1998). Two of the vessels are newly built with a capacity of 160 trailers each and the remaining vessel has an age of six years with a capacity of 66 trailers. Since the Port of Istanbul is busy and rather congested at times, the Port of Tekirdag was selected for this line taking into account its advantages in terms of waiting times at the port and access to the country whilst avoiding the heavy sea traffic that characterises the straits of Bosphorus close to Istanbul.

In addition to ro-ro services between Italy and Turkey, new service lines have also developed between a number of Turkish ports and Constantza in Romania, Novorossisk and Yalta in the Ukraine, Soci in Georgia and Ilicevsk in the Black Sea area with a fleet of 12 ro-ro vessels. Currently, ro-ro shipping in Turkey continues to develop year by year on the basis of an expansion of liner and regular shipping services in the Eastern Mediterranean and Black Sea markets.

Ferry services Much of the discussion on the ferry market in the Eastern Mediterranean area, and the Italy-Greece-Turkey corridor in particular, has already been completed in an earlier section and it was clear from this that it remains another considerably active shipping market for Turkey, which has gained in importance following the civil war in the former Yugoslavia, which broke out at the beginning of the 1990s. As was noted during the discussion on the conceptual contexts, the passengers for this market have come largely from the 2.5 million Turkish people living in various Central and Western European countries, dominated by those domiciled in Germany (Ministry of Labour and Social Security, 1996) and visiting their families and relatives in Turkey particularly in the summer (European Commission, 1996). These people, who as we have seen, previously travelled to and from Turkey by road, have had to change transport mode to either air or sea transport because of the impossibility of road transport throughout much of the former Yugoslavia territory. Therefore, as a result, a dramatic increase in the traffic volume of sea transport in this corridor has been recorded up until recently (Cruise and Ferry Info, 1994) aiming to by-pass the conflict (LSM, 1994).

In addition to the rapidly developing ferry market in the Eastern Mediterranean, the ferry market in the Black Sea has also been showing marked activity after the collapse of the Former Soviet Union (FSU). A number of ferry operators have started to operate in an increasing trend year by year on the lines between the ports of Turkey and the new FSU countries. Most of the passengers in this market place have been contributing to the national economies of their countries by carrying goods in their personal luggage as exports and imports acting as a form of unregistered commerce, commonly termed as 'luggage trading'. A recent estimate of the contribution to the Turkish economy through this type of trading was an approximate value of US$ 8 billion in 1997; however, it remains a 'black' trade that is not included within the national economic indicators.

The impact of the private sector upon the shipping industry

Initially, the place of the private sector within the shipping industry in Turkey is explained in this section. We then go on to compare the private sector with the state owned and operated institutions from the public sector. Secondly, privatisation actions taking place within the Turkish shipping industry since the beginning of the 1990s are also noted and analysed for their contribution to the sector as a whole.

The private sector in the shipping industry

The majority of the institutions, organisations and companies in the Turkish shipping industry and the vessels in the merchant fleet are owned and operated by organisations in the private sector. Approximately 95% of maritime institutions belong to the private sector, the details of which we noted earlier in the discussion of the social context. Approximately 77% of the vessels were owned and operated by private companies by the end of 1996 with approximately the same percentage also the case in 1997. Tables 25 and 26 illustrate the total number of vessels and the total tonnage of the fleet owned and operated by the private and public sectors, respectively. Their percentages in the total merchant fleet are also illustrated in the same tables. In addition to those indicators, some 77% of the total number of vessels, representing approximately 94% of the total tonnage in dwt, was owned and operated by the private sector in the shipping industry in 1997, which is a very considerable amount indicating the dominance of this sector. The percentages were approximately the same in 1996 illustrating very little change in the figures during this time.

The majority of the Turkish shipping industry thus lies within the private sector and benefits from the dynamism of the entrepreneurial character that remains a major characteristic. The management system of these companies and the methods of business operation are based upon the principles that typify a highly competitive free market situation. The majority of the shipping industry receives its dynamism and progressive characteristics from this private sector where those involved in the maritime sector are required to stand on their own feet. This enterprising character has been adopted widely in undertaking new projects and in sustaining an active shipping market in Turkey. The individual private shipowners and ship operators tend to have healthy balance sheets and relatively prosperous financial situations. As a result of this, the Turkish merchant fleet has started to modernise and invest in the future by obtaining larger and more modern vessels, in particular a number of recently built container vessels, which will further facilitate competition with other operators across the world.

In addition, the majority of the Turkish shipowners and ship operators are shipping related families for more than five generations. Therefore, their experience and practice in the shipping market play an important role in generating dynamism in the market place for the Turkish shipping industry.

Table 25
Sector distribution of the Turkish merchant fleet by total number of vessels (31.12.1997)

Vessel type	PRIVATE SECTOR		PUBLIC SECTOR	
	Total	% of tonnage	Total	% of tonnage
Bulk carrier	168	14	13	1.1
General cargo	454	37.9	15	1.3
Tanker	90	7.5	8	0.7
OBO	8	0.6	--	--
Ro-ro & Ferry	31	2.6	11	0.9
Container	11	0.9	--	--
Others	154	12.9	235	19.6
TOTAL	**915**	**76.4**	**282**	**23.6**

Source: Chamber of Shipping (1998a).

Shipowners and ship operators do not receive any direct subsidies or financial aid from the Government; on the contrary, they survive and trade on their own within the strict confines of the national liberalisation policy. A number of issues have been taken up by the Government with the aim of improving the merchant fleet, and these include investment in inland waterway shipping, Black Sea shipping, the construction of container vessels etc. However, this encouragement goes no further than promises of the Government with no further steps in terms of either direct financial aid or indirect support. Therefore, it is reasonable to conclude that the dynamism in the private sector in the Turkish shipping industry is the force that acts in making the shipping industry one of the most significant and progressive industries within the Turkish economy.

Table 26
Sector distribution of the Turkish merchant fleet by total tonnages (million dwt) (31.12.1997)

Vessel type	PRIVATE SECTOR		PUBLIC SECTOR	
	Total	%	Total	%
Bulk carrier	6.44	60.9	0.41	4.0
General cargo	1.31	12.4	0.11	1.0
Tanker	0.90	8.5	0.05	0.4
OBO	0.82	7.7	--	--
Ro-ro & Ferry	0.15	1.4	0.02	0.2
Container	0.09	0.9	--	--
Others	0.19	1.9	0.07	0.7
TOTAL	**9.90**	**93.7**	**0.66**	**6.3**

Source: Chamber of Shipping (1998a).

Thus the private sector of the Turkish shipping industry receives no subsidies - in terms of direct financial support - from the government for the development of the merchant fleet. Therefore, shipowners and ship operators finance investment themselves from their own capital or take loans from foreign international institutions at their own risk. For example, a recent and very sizeable loan received was a total of US$ 250 million from Japan (Drewry, 1995). This loan was shared by a number of shipowners and shipbuilders under the auspicious of the Turkish Chamber of Shipping located in Istanbul.

Meanwhile, contrary to this, a regulation for the protection of the national merchant fleet was brought by the government to place a priority upon vessels placed under Turkish flags for carrying import goods for state owned companies located in the public sector. In addition, the Turkish Chamber of Shipping issued a report stating that tankers under Turkish flags should carry a greater proportion of Turkey's oil imports and thus secure a greater share in the country's foreign trade. In addition, there has been a further protection policy to carry at least half of the imported oil by vessels under Turkish flags with the objective of further contributing to the economic prosperity of the country.

Partly as a consequence of the shipping industry not receiving direct support from the Government, it has become more assertive and undoubtedly more internationally minded since the beginning of the 1990s (Seatrade Review, 1997). This was reflected in the comments of the president of the Turkish

71

Chamber of Shipping who emphasised that the shipping community had far exceeded Government levels of activity and initiative represented by the dynamic entrepreneurship which was characteristic of the industry.

The organisational and managerial characteristics of Turkish private shipping companies also match the dynamic free market conditions that typify the sector, in which very high levels of competition take place. Decision making and responsibility are shared amongst top management, company staff and workers within the recently established private shipping companies. On the contrary, there are some contrasts to this within some of the more private and individual shipping family companies, where decision making rests entirely within the structure of family members which make up the top management.

It is clear that there has developed substantial differences between state and privately owned and operated maritime institutions and companies in Turkey. As a consequence, further privatisation actions are now important in sustaining any further developments that might occur within this industry.

Privatisation within the Turkish shipping industry

Privatisation has been a popular political tool during the elections in Turkey; however, recently it has continued to focus upon the promises of politicians rather than substantial actions. Despite this, some privatisation actions have been emphasised and highlighted within government policies through a number of policies and regulations.

Privatisation actions, which commenced in 1985 as part of the liberalisation policy for the economy, have continued until 1997 with an approximate average of US$ 400 million annually totalling US$ 3.5 billion between 1985 and 1997 and look set to continue into the future. A total of 165 state owned institutions have been privatised since 1985 covering some of the biggest state owned public institutions including Turkish Telecom, IsBank, Petrol Office, Tupras Petrol Refinery and Havas Airport Services whilst further privatisation actions continue within some of these organisations plus a number of others.

The managerial organisation of state owned maritime institutions and companies tends to suffer from a very heavy bureaucracy and decision making commonly rests only with the top management as noted earlier. Moreover, heavy losses have continued to be posted for many years at most of the state owned and operated maritime companies. Therefore, privatisation actions within the maritime sector have been on the agenda of the Government since the beginning of the 1990s; however so far, very few direct steps have been taken by the Government and privatisation actions have remained only as promises stifled by the slow progress of government procedures.

The broad privatisation programme includes a number of maritime institutions, and in particular the four major shipyards and three small state owned shipyards situated in Istanbul and Izmir, various ports and the national cargo carrier and national ferry operator - both owned and operated by the Turkish Maritime Organisation (Lloyd's List, 1994; Uysal and Mazgit, 1996). However, the plans for maritime privatisation have hit many problems with company sales falling far behind the proposed government privatisation timetable.

Recently, priority was supposed to have been given to the privatisation of these state owned and operated maritime institutions following the new regulation brought by the Undersecretariat of Shipping (1997). In addition, the Undersecretariat included the Privatisation Administration on a list of institutions to become more active in their relations with the maritime sector in the hope of encouraging greater co-ordination in the necessary related legal and administrative activities.

A total of US$ 12.5 billion revenue from privatisation actions was targeted for 1998 (Forum, 1998). On behalf of the maritime industry, privatisation of the Turkish Maritime Organisation was highlighted as the major event and has been handled separately by a special department of the Prime Ministry. A detailed financial analysis of the organisation has been undertaken by independent financial auditors. Privatisation actions for properties and vessels of Turkish Maritime Lines - the major ferry operator, and Turkish Cargo Lines - the major cargo carrier, both owned by the Turkish Maritime Organisation, a number of ports owned and operated by the Turkish Maritime Organisation and some shipyards owned and operated by the Turkish Ship Industry, are still under progress and are targeted to be completed by the beginning of 1999. Vessels owned and operated by state institutions, which are still under progress of privatisation actions, are as follows:

> Turkish Maritime Lines: four ferries operating on international lines (in the Eastern Mediterranean, in particular), four ferries and four passenger vessels operating on national domestic lines;
> Turkish Cargo Lines: 16 general cargo vessels totalling 172,371 dwt, nine dry bulk carriers totalling 345,961 dwt and four ro-ro vessels totalling 49,551 grt (Forum, 1997).

The sale of the national cargo carrier was approved by the Privatisation High Council at the beginning of 1997; however, although there was a successful bidder, there have been constant rumours emerging from the Privatisation Administration about insufficient payment by the buyers caused by rises in the total amount due from US$ 205 million to US$ 223 million resulting from additional interest payments (Seatrade Review, 1997). Consequently, negotiations were delayed to a later date until another successful bidder could be found. The national cargo carrier as one of the major shipping companies, is a much slimmed down organisation compared with its earlier condition during the beginning of the 1990s and currently is the owner and operator of 29 vessels and much other valuable property and land. However, this state owned company has little hope of contributing to the national economy given its current situation with vessels which require fundamental refurbishment and modernisation.

Privatisation of the major ports is expected centred around the idea of the privatisation of secondary ports encouraging the major ones to follow suit. The ports already privatised by 1997 are the Port of Tekirdag on the Sea of Marmara and the Ports of Sinop, Ordu, Giresun, Rize and Hopa on the Black Sea. These ports were previously owned and operated by the Turkish Maritime Organisation and are currently leased to and operated by the Tekirdag Port Organisation, the Port Organisations of Sinop, Ordu and Giresun established by Cakiroglu Building and Construction, Rize Port Organisation and Investment established by three shipping groups - Yardimci, Ergencler and Cillioglu, and Park Shipping and Hopa Port Organisation (Chamber of Shipping, 1998c). Bidding for privatisation of the Port of Antalya currently owned by the Turkish Maritime Organisation, was cancelled after a series of negotiations in May 1998 and was delayed until a successful bidder could be found in the nearest future (International Transport News, 1998).

Consequently, the future of privatisation actions in the maritime sector is still unclear. The need for privatisation of Turkish ports has been highlighted continuously by the Turkish Chamber of Shipping because of an insufficient level of productivity, insufficient use of technological equipment, the out-of-date equipment, heavy bureaucracy and overload of paperwork, the lack of computerised processing, insufficient training for operators of technical equipment, the inexpert nature at managerial levels and the unnecessary intervention of some politicians in the decision-making process that tends to occur.

Major shipping companies

Major shipping companies in Turkey are mostly groups of medium size companies with family links, each company the owner and operator of a fleet of between three and ten vessels. The majority of them are currently located in Istanbul - the heart of foreign and domestic trade in the country - with many of them originated from the Black Sea coasts from the beginning of the 1900s. Having developed in parallel to the development of world trade in general, the Turkish shipping industry is mostly composed of private shipping companies or groups of companies, as noted earlier. There is an approximate total of 2,500 shipowners in Turkey employing approximately 100,000 people (The Economist, 1995).

The top 14 companies or groups of companies according to their total tonnages at the beginning of 1995 and 1998 are illustrated in Tables 27 and 28, respectively. Also illustrated in both tables, are the positions of Turkish Cargo Lines, the Cerrahogullari Group, the Kaptanoglu Group, the Kalkavan Group and the Sohtorik Group at the head of the lists of top companies illustrating their stability in terms of importance in the market place. In the range of private companies, Turkish Cargo Lines is the only state owned and operated company to be found and is placed at the top of the list in Table 27. Despite representing the 2nd of all companies and the 1st amongst the private shipping companies on the same list in 1995, Marti Shipping Group went bankrupt in 1997 after four of their vessels were involved in accidents, although some of its associated companies are still operating in the agency, freight forwarding and shipbroking areas of the industry.

Turkish Cargo Lines

The fleet of Turkish Cargo Lines consisted of 40 vessels totalling 810,709 dwt during 1996; however, this figure decreased in 1997 following the objective of the management group of the company to improve the quality of the fleet. Turkish Cargo Lines is currently the owner and operator of a fleet consisting of 16 general cargo vessels totalling 172,371 dwt, nine dry bulk carriers totalling 345,961 dwt and four ro-ro vessels totalling 49,551 grt aggregating to a fleet of a total of 537,173 dwt with 29 vessels (Forum, 1997; Turkish Cargo Lines, 1998).

Table 27

The major shipping companies in terms of total tonnages in 1995

Company	Total number of vessels	Total tonnage (dwt)
1. Turkish Cargo Lines	40	810,709
2. Marti Shipping	6	645,000
3. Zihni Shipping	5	502,083
4. Um Shipping	3	457,197
5. Dunya Shipping	3	430,706
6. Denizcilik Shipping	7	351,600
7. Kalkavanlar Shipping Group	13	334,909
8. Cerrahogullari Shipping Group	3	269,354
9. Kaptanoglu Shipping Group	12	214,093
10. Colakoglu Shipping	4	213,777
11. Cerrahgil Shipping Group	4	211,198
12. Kasif Kalkavan Shipping Group	7	167,385
13. Semih Sohtorik Shipping Group	5	138,969
14. Sohtorik Shipping Group	5	114,546

Source: The Economist (1995).

Table 28

The major shipping companies in terms of total tonnages at the beginning of 1998

Company	Total tonnage (dwt)
1. Turkish Cargo Lines	537,173
2. Semih Sohtorik Shipping Group	497,597
3. Colakoglu Shipping	489,043
4. Erol Yucel of Marti Shipping	459,916
5. S Umut Shipping	450,034
6. Kaptanoglu Shipping Group	383,211
7. Sadan Kalkavan Shipping Group	356,992
8. Pak and Ziler Shipping	330,202
9. Aslan Shipping	321,670
10. Ihsan Kalkavan Shipping Group	278,979
11. Cerrahoglu Shipping Group	251,932
12. Ozcelik and Bahtinur Shipping	248,100

Sources: The World (1998a); Chamber of Shipping (1998b).

The top 40 maritime companies or groups of companies in terms of their contribution to the national economy in 1995, are illustrated in Table 29. The top two companies and the 14th company are the only state owned and operated companies with the top two companies currently undergoing the process of privatisation action. The first company - the Turkish Maritime Organisation - is the owner and operator of a number of secondary ports and is also the owner of Turkish Maritime Lines, the major ferry owner and operator, and Turkish Cargo Lines, the major cargo carrier. The 14th biggest company in terms of its contribution to the national economy is the Turkish State Railways, which is the owner and operator of the major seven ports in the country - the Ports of Istanbul, Izmir, Mersin, Iskenderun, Derince, Samsun and Bandirma.

Turkish Cargo Lines operates in both the conventional general cargo and dry bulk markets as well as liner container lines as follows:

> *Mediterranean container line:* Valencia-Barcelona - Marseilles - La Spezia - Piraeus - Izmir - Istanbul
>
> *Eastern Mediterranean container line:* Alexandria - Beirut - Mersin - Izmir - Istanbul
>
> *Southern Mediterranean container line:* Rades (Tunisia) - Izmir - Istanbul
>
> *Northern Europe conventional cargo line - 1:* Antwerp - Hamburg - Bremen - Immingham - Izmir - Derince - Istanbul
>
> *Northern Europe conventional cargo line - 2:* Antwerp - Hamburg - Bremen - Immingham - Gdansk - Mersin - Izmir - Derince - Istanbul
>
> *Black Sea Ro-Ro line:* Constantza - Derince
>
> *Mediterranean Ro-Ro line:* Trieste - Cesme (Izmir) - Istanbul
>
> *Far East conventional cargo line:* Kobe - Yokohama - Pusan - Izmir - Istanbul
>
> *America express container line:* New York - Baltimore - Charleston - Norfolk - Izmir - Istanbul
>
> *America conventional cargo line:* New York - Baltimore - Charleston - Norfolk - Izmir - Istanbul.

Table 29

Top 40 Turkish maritime companies 1995

Company	Contribution (US$ million)
1. Turkish Maritime Organisation	161,127
2. Turkish Cargo Lines	127,698
3. Marti Holding	80,593
4. Colakoglu Metal Industry	63,496
5. Kaptanoglu Shipping Group	57,669
6. Marti Vessel Leasing	53,308
7. UND Shipping Group	44,186
8. Tempo Shipping Group	41,894
9. Cerrahgil Shipping Group	41,230
10. Sadan Kalkavan Shipping Group	35,018
11. Ekmar Shipping Group	28,905
12. Antuvan Makzume International Transport	26,529
13. Arkas Shipping and Transport	25,923
14. Turkish State Railways	25,643
15. Zihni Holding	25,270
16. Aslan Transmarine Shipping Group	24,269
17. Sark Express Shipping Group	23,890
18. Ditas Shipping Group	23,214
19. Master Shipping Group	22,741
20. Diler Shipping Group	22,017
21. Yardimci Shipping Group	21,831
22. Dunya Shipping Group	21,549
23. Kasif Kalkavan Shipping Group	21,281
24. Altinel Plastic Industry	21,256
25. Bamtrans International Transport	20,174
26. Semih Sohtorik Shipping Group	20,036
27. Marmara Transport and Shipping Group	19,558
28. Transbosphore Shipping Industry	18,570
29. Selim Sohtorik Shipping Group	18,357
30. Cemre Shipping Group	18,164
31. Ulusoy Shipping Group	17,421
32. Genel Shipping Group	17,235
33. Basco Shipping	16,542
34. Mardas Shipping Group	15,437
35. Mobil Oil - Turk Company	15,023
36. Pamfilya Tourism and Traveling Company	14,901
37. Sayinsoy Shipping Group	14,796
38. Bedri Ince Shipping Group	14,685
39. Maurice and Hendrick Dutilh Company	14,003
40. Denizcilik Shipping	13,550

Sources: International Trade News (1996); Forum (1997).

As we also noted earlier, Turkish Cargo Lines is now within the process of privatisation actions. The highest bid put forward was for a total of US$ 141.3 million in 1997; however, negotiations were delayed until a later date in 1998. Some of the bidders included Marti Holding, a group of 20 shipowners and the 'Group of Turkish Cargo Lines Common Entrepreneurship' of which 51% is owned by a union of 1,200 managers and workers of Turkish Cargo Lines and 49% by Mr Dalan - former Major of Istanbul and also former Member of the Turkish Parliament. The company has still not yet been totally privatised.

Marti Holding

The 3rd top company and also placed at the top of the private companies at the time was Marti Holding as the owner and operator of a fleet of six vessels totalling 645,000 dwt in 1995 (The Economist, 1995), which reached ten vessels totalling 1,050,000 dwt in 1996 (Forum, 1997). The companies within the Holding also dealt with shipbroking, chartering, freight forwarding, agency services and insurance areas of the shipping industry. Marti Holding was also the owner of a steel manufacturing company and a logistics company with a fleet of ten trucks. However, the holding went bankrupt in 1996, but Erol Yucel Shipping Company - owned by the former chairman of Marti Holding - is still active (see Table 28, the 4th company) within the liner agency, land transportation, freight forwarding and container services areas of the shipping industry in conjunction with other partners also working in similar areas in the industry.

The Shipping Groups of Cerrahgil, Kalkavan, Kaptanoglu and Sohtorik

As also illustrated in Table 29, most of the shipping companies are "groups of companies", which were expanded and grouped within sister companies after the liberalisation policy in the national economy after the 1980s. The Kaptanoglu Shipping Group, Cerrahgil Shipping Group, Kalkavan Shipping Group, Zihni Shipping Group, UND Shipping Group, Yardimci Group etc. are some examples of these shipping groups of companies.

These shipping groups are some of the major groups of shipping companies sharing a considerable percentage of the merchant fleet for a very long time, also illustrated in Tables 27, 28 and 29. Management groups of these companies play an important role in decision-making for the improvement and future of Turkish shipping by also participating in and managing the Chamber of Shipping. For example, Mr Cengiz Kaptanoglu - Chairman of the Kaptanoglu Shipping Group with a fleet of 383,211 dwt, is also the Chairman of the Chamber of Shipping alongside Mr Esref Cerrahoglu - Chairman of the Cerrahgil Shipping Group with a fleet of 251,932 dwt, as the Counsellor of the Chamber of Shipping.

Turkon Line

Turkon Line is a newly established company as a sister company of one of the shipping groups of companies of the Kalkavan family and its role was outlined in an earlier section. The company concentrates upon liner container shipping in the Mediterranean, Eastern Mediterranean and American liner markets with a total fleet of eight vessels at an average of two years totalling 71,680 dwt. As the first Turkish company operating its own fleet of fully container vessels in the liner market, Turkon Line is one of the more significant and developing companies based upon its contribution to the Turkish shipping industry.

UND Shipping Group

Turkey, as a landbridge between Eastern and South-Eastern Europe and the Middle East, has a significant geographical position in the area. The civil war in the former Yugoslavia and the Gulf crisis in the Middle East at the beginning of the 1990s caused a serious crisis for land transport companies and freight forwarders in Turkey. As a result, the Association of International Land Transporters (UND), with a total of some 690 members, demanded an increase in the total capacity of ro-ro vessels of Turkish Cargo Lines operating in the Italy-Turkey corridor in the Eastern Mediterranean to act as a by-pass for the land transport routes that used to pass through Greece and the former Yugoslavia. As a result, the UND Shipping Group of Companies was established in 1993 by 47 members of the Association in the form of two sister shipping companies. A shipping pool was created by Turkish Cargo Lines and the UND Shipping Group operating a total of eight ro-ro vessels - four each, two acquired by UND in each of 1994 and 1995 - between Trieste in Italy and Istanbul and Izmir in Turkey (Cargo News, 1998; The Economist, 1995). The UND Shipping Group has benefited as a result of this rapidly developing shipping trade route since the early 1990s, and currently is one of the leading groups of companies in this region with an additional 9th vessel on the order list. Hauliers use the line for services between the United Kingdom, France, Belgium, the Netherlands, Luxembourg and Germany to Turkey, the Middle East and beyond and in so doing now avoid many of the problems associated with transport through the former Yugoslavia, Romania and Bulgaria. The total amount of investment for the fleet was around US$ 400 million from which 35% was received from an international loan from the World Bank (The World, 1998a).

Some of the companies or groups of companies on the list of the highest contributors to the national economy in Table 29 have also been major dealers in other commercial areas - such as general transport, logistics, shipbuilding, the steel industry, the food industry and tourism, in addition to their shipping business. For example, steel and metal manufacturer Colakoglu Metal Industry also deals with container manufacturing, owns and operates its own port and carries its products by its fleet in the international markets; the UND Shipping Group, the Bamtrans International Transport Company, Marmara Transport-Shipping Group and Ulusoy Shipping Group are some examples of the major transport, logistics and freight forwarding groups of companies; The Association of Ship Building Industrialists, the Yardimci Shipping Group and the Sedef Ship Industry are in the shipbuilding industry with Yardimci Shipping Group as a shipowner, shipbuilder and a shipyard owner and Sedef Ship Industry as a shipbuilder and a shipyard owner; Pamfilya Tourism and Traveling Company mainly deals with the tourism industry as well as serving passenger transport.

Contribution to the national economy

The Turkish maritime business is not limited to the borders of Turkey and naturally enough, has links with the world seas. Consequently, the maritime industry is a major contributor to the Turkish economy through external relations and through its potential to earn hard currency. International income from the shipping industry amounted to nearly US$ 3.5 billion in foreign exchange in 1994. As a point of comparison, US$ 4.2 billion was earned by the Turkish tourism industry in 1994. The income of the maritime industry reached US$ 5 billion in 1995 and was universally considered to be an important figure for the Turkish economy. The contribution of the maritime industry to the Turkish economy was targeted to be US$ 5 billion again for 1996 (Chamber of Shipping, 1996c) and exceeded this, reaching US$ 6 billion for 1996 with a merchant fleet of 10.89 million dwt (Chamber of Shipping, 1996f).

The Turkish GNP was US$ 175 billion in 1995 and the contribution of shipping to the GNP was 2.9%. The GNP was forecast as US$ 181 billion for 1996 with the share of shipping as 2.8% (AIIB, 1996). The GNP was actually US$ 173.1 in 1996 but the share contributed by the shipping industry towards the Turkish GNP actually reached 3.5% in that same year with a contribution of US$ 6 billion (Chamber of Shipping, 1996f). Similarly, the contribution was a total of US$ 6.5 billion in 1997 (Chamber of Shipping, 1998a), although it was targeted to be US$ 7 billion. It is forecast that the merchant fleet will reach a capacity of 15 million dwt at the end of the 1990s. The contribution of shipping to the Turkish economy by that time is forecast to be US$ 10 billion with a merchant fleet of 20 million dwt by the beginning of the year 2000 (Chamber of Shipping, 1996c).

These indicators are insufficient in comparison with the major European maritime countries such as Greece and Norway. For instance, the Greek fleet increased to 120 million dwt in 1993 bringing a total income of US$ 44 billion, which to put it into context, is equal to 10% of the reserves of the ten wealthiest countries in the world. Nevertheless, although the income to Turkey is relatively small by comparison, it remains of great value particularly in the light of the country's other international earnings and its status as a pseudo-developing country.

Many industrial and commercial sectors were highly affected by the economic crisis in Turkey which took place in 1994. In particular, a number of small shipping companies were affected at the beginning of 1994 with some vessels waiting in Istanbul Bosphorus for two or three weeks looking for employment. However, they largely recovered during the second half of 1994. On the other hand, none of the bigger shipowners and ship operators were noticeably affected by the economic crisis because they commonly operated their vessels for shipments between third countries and thus, had plenty of opportunities for earning hard currency (Chamber of Shipping, 1996c).

As a consequence, a total of US$ 10 billion contribution of the shipping industry to the economy is forecast by the Turkish Chamber of Shipping for the year 2000. Annual contributions of the Turkish shipping industry to the national economy - including forecast contributions until the year 2000 - are illustrated in Table 30. The contribution of shipping to the Turkish economy was US$ 6 billion in 1996, whilst the role of shipping was US$ 300 billion within the world economy (Chamber of Shipping, 1996f). As a consequence, the Turkish shipping industry as a contributor to the national economy of Turkey equated to 2% of shipping's contribution to the world economy at that time.

Turkish shipping - the current situation

By way of concluding this chapter, it is proposed to assess the current (1998) situation that exists in the Turkish shipping sector. This will then provide a basis for the discussion to follow in later chapters, of the position of shipping policy and its relationship to the current infrastructure and activity.

Table 30
Annual contribution of the shipping industry to the national economy (US$ billion)

Year	Total amount of contribution (US$ billion)
1994	3.5
1995	5.0
1996	6.0
1997	6.5
1998	8.0
1999	9.0
2000	10.0

Sources: Chamber of Shipping (1996e), (1996f), (1998a).

Under the current Six Year Plan of the Turkish government the Turkish fleet had reached some 11 million dwt by early 1998 with annual earnings of around US$ 5 million. Future plans envisage an annual fleet increase of about 1 million dwt.

On the 1st January of 1998 there were 1197 ships registered in Turkey which were over 150grt which is an increase of around 45% since 1987 and thus a sizeable achievement. The government plans to increase this figure to 15 million dwt and a foreign currency earning of 10 billion US$ by the year 2000. This previous growth and the optimistic plans that exist stem from the development in management of the fleet and by the ship owning and operating companies which now receive almost no subsidy and have extended their international links so that they are now the most international of all Turkish industries. Some 93% of both imports and exports in 1998 will travel by sea.

In terms of specific trade, in 1997 some 57% of Turkey's seaborne export trade was with European Union countries, whilst a further 24% was with Islamic countries. However, the situation for imports is rather different in that only 14% emerges from the EU, whilst 37% comes from the Islamic Countries and 8% from the USA. Trading activities with the Black Sea Economic Co-operation Countries increased by 29% from 18.3 million tons in 1996 to 23.6 million tons in 1997 with the largest trading partner for Turkey being The Russian Federation.

Meanwhile, the share of foreign seaborne trade carried on Turkish vessels is shown in Table 31 which reflects a decline in Turkish flag involvement both

83

in percentage and tons carried, contrasting with the overall increase in the tonnage of exports and imports for the country as a whole. Turkish oil imports are dominated by overseas carriers with less than 5% carried by Turkish registered vessels, a situation widely condemned in Turkey but which is unlikely to change without state interference in the market place. The possibility of this is increasing with the proposals for the new second registry to encourage ship owners not to flag out their vessels.

Table 31
Turkish flag share of seaborne trade (million tons)

Year	Total	Export	Import	Tons	%
1994	74.743	22.113	52.631	36.986	49
1995	84.141	20.175	64.007	35.157	42
1996	91.680	18.846	72.834	36.058	39
1997	112.373	37.009	75.364	32.835	29

Source: Authors

Container exports reflect these trends somewhat in that exports in 1997 reached 352,559 TEUs and imports 400,679 TEUs. The large majority of these containers were carried by overseas operators with the limited exceptions of the Turkish container shipping operators noted above who now possess some 15 vessels. Container movements were limited to activities at Mersin, Iskenderun, Samsun, Izmir, Derince, Bandirma, Istanbul, Armaport, Gemport and Sedef.

The average age of the Turkish fleet of 1500 dwt and above is now around 17 years. The majority of vessels purchased by Turkish shipowners remain second-hand acquisitions and these purchases have been buoyant since the mid 1990s onwards.

From all this we can see that Turkish shipping remains a significant world player despite the pressures it faces in common with many other traditional fleets. It has an active ports sector and the industry as a whole is undergoing considerable development with the new registry, privatisation policies and the growth of maritime activities.

In the next chapter we shall turn specifically to the Turkish ports situation and their relationship to the shipping industry.

4. Major ports in Turkey

Introduction

Ports in Turkey consist of 15 major government ports, approximately 50 more small piers under the control of municipalities and approximately 60 private ports and piers. The major ports under the control of the government are either owned and operated by Turkish State Railways or by the Turkish Maritime Organisation. Seven general purpose major ports, which are owned and operated by Turkish State Railways and thus indirectly under the control of the Ministry of Transport, are the Ports of Istanbul (also sometimes known as the Port of Haydarpasa), Derince and Bandirma on the Sea of Marmara to the northwest of the country, the Port of Izmir on the Aegean Sea to the west, the Ports of Mersin and Iskenderun on the Mediterranean Sea to the south and the Port of Samsun on the Black Sea to the north of the country.

The remaining eight government ports, which are considered secondary major ports, are actually owned, managed and operated by the Turkish Maritime Organisation and are situated as follows: the Port of Tekirdag on the Sea of Marmara to the northwest, the Ports of Sinop, Ordu, Giresun, Trabzon, Rize and Hopa on the Black Sea to the north and the Port of Antalya on the Mediterranean Sea to the south of the country. In addition to these ports, there are also six other ports within this organisation, which are considerably less significant compared with the others: the Ports of Dikili, Cesme, Kusadasi, Gulluk and Marmaris on the Aegean Sea and the Port of Alanya on the Mediterranean Sea.

These state owned and operated ports are ports which offer a full range of services which includes amongst other facilities and activities, pilotage and towage, quay occupation, fresh water supply, solid and liquid waste removal, handling services, storage, commodity weighing and the rental of equipment. Stevedoring services are mostly supplied by the port authority and the existence of a private stevedoring service is not allowed at most of the state ports. Port tariffs are calculated by the Turkish Maritime Organisation and port charges may slightly differ from one port to another. A vessel calling at a port in Turkey is charged for pilotage (both entering and leaving the port), tugging (in/out of port), quay dues, waste removal, sanitary dues, light dues (again both entering and leaving the port), a chamber of shipping fee, an agency fee, an attendance/supervision fee and a number of other charges depending upon the types of cargoes loaded and unloaded, i.e. transshipment fee, a commission on inward freight, freight tax, forwarding fees, harbour dues etc.

Ports under the control of municipalities tend to be comparatively small and are limited to a small volume of coastal traffic serving the local needs of coastal cities and towns. The majority of these ports are situated either to the north or northwest with 20 of them on the Black Sea and 17 of them on the Sea of Marmara, with the remaining seven on the Aegean Sea and six on the Mediterranean Sea.

The third group of ports are privately owned with the majority of them classified as special purpose ports and piers serving the needs of industrial plants, in particular. The majority of private ports, constituting approximately 40 in number, are situated on the Sea of Marmara to the northwest of the country where the region is heavily dominated with industrial plants, with the remaining eight on the Mediterranean Sea, seven on the Black Sea and five on the Aegean Sea.

Recent total trade indicators including both foreign trades and cabotage shipping activities to and from all of these ports in Turkey are illustrated in Table 32. In addition to the total trade indicators, total trade undertaken to/from these ports in 1997 was 168.8 million tons including transit shipping of 14.7 million tons (Chamber of Shipping, 1998a).

Major state owned ports

Approximately 90% of the total cargo handled at state owned ports in Turkey is handled at the Ports of the Turkish State Railways (TSR). All of these ports have links with land and railway transportation routes and some are even positioned close to airports i.e. the Ports of Istanbul and Izmir, which make them all ideally displaced from a logistical point of view. In addition, all these state owned ports have been traditional crossing points for trading and cultural activities between the two continents of Europe and Asia. As a consequence, these ports act as the major gateways for the country to the world, whilst playing a key role in the international and domestic transportation systems and foreign trades of Turkey.

Table 32
Total trades undertaken to/from ports in Turkey ('000 tons)

Year	Imports (unloading)	Exports (loading)	Cabotage	TOTAL
1993	60,003	17,379	34,313	**111,695**
1994	48,805	20,932	31,905	**101,641**
1995	58,502	19,760	32,709	**110,971**
1996	65,290	18,035	34,208	**117,533**
1997	75,363	37,009	41,728	**154,100**

Source: Chamber of Shipping (1998a).

Ports of the Turkish State Railways have a 30 million ton capacity for cargo handling with a 34 million ton annual capacity of general cargo storage and a container storage capacity of 1,080,000 TEUs/year. 16,420 ships can be accommodated annually by these ports with a total berth capacity of 50 million tons based upon a continuous three-shift operation system. Approximately 34 million tons of cargo are handled annually at these ports with the majority of cargo types being dry bulk, general cargo and containers. The general specifications of these ports are illustrated in brief in Table 35. In addition, the total cargo handled at these ports between 1993-1997 is illustrated in Table 32. Furthermore, the Ports of Istanbul, Izmir and Mersin are analysed in this section in some detail because of their crucial importance to the Turkish economy and their relative significance compared with other ports.

In addition to the equipment currently utilised at the Ports of the Turkish State Railways, a loan totaling US$ 85 million negotiated from the European Investment Bank (EIB), was borrowed by the managers of the ports for the improvement and upgrading of the equipment which was available (Interview, 1998). The equipment which will be purchased for use at the Ports of Istanbul, Izmir and Mersin is listed as follows:

35 container mobile cranes,
1 gantry crane,
35 empty container forklifts,
26 yard cranes,
43 tugmasters,
86 trailers,
33 x 3-ton diesel forklifts, and
22 x 2.5-ton battery forklifts.

Port of Istanbul (Port of Haydarpasa)

The Port of Istanbul is situated in the city centre of the most industrialised and the biggest metropolitan city in Turkey. The port is connected by both land and rail transport modes to its surrounding hinterland, located on the Sea of Marmara and as we noted earlier, even has links with air transport through the international airport which is 27 kms away from the port.

The port, which is characterised as one of the few ports with a sizeable and well developed container terminal in the country, has 17 berths with a total length of 2,675 metres and has a vessel calling capacity of 2,213 vessels/year and a container handling capacity of 354,000 TEUs/year. The port is a well equipped modern container port with large storage areas and skilled personnel. Container vessels can access four berths of more than 600 metres length and load and unload containers using four gantry cranes. The container terminal also offers reefer facilities allowing a continuous service for refrigerated containers. In addition to the special ro-ro berth and terminal, the container berths can also accommodate ro-ro vessels and ferries at times of high demand. A specific container freight station is used for LCL containers. General cargo berths allow simultaneous mooring of 14 vessels. Floating vessels comprise one floating crane of 250 tons capacity, five tugboats, three rail ferries and three mooring boats. Bulk cargo is handled with high capacity pneumatic equipment and can be stored in a silo of 34,000 tons capacity via a conveyor system. All variety of commodities are stored in warehouses and in open areas facilitated by sophisticated control systems and an efficient port security service. It is aimed that a flexible and reliable service should be supplied 24 hours a day and 365 days a year.

Details of port capacities of the Port of Istanbul, total major cargo handled between 1993-1997 and cargo handling equipment of the port are illustrated in Tables 34, 36 and 37.

Port of Izmir

The Port of Izmir is situated in the city centre of the second industrialised and the second biggest metropolitan city in Turkey. The port is connected with both road and rail transport modes and lies on the coast of the Aegean Sea and even has good links with air transport through the local international airport which is approximately 25 kms away from the port.

Table 33
Total cargo handled at the ports of Turkish State Railways between 1993 and 1997 ('000 tons)

Port of TSR	1993	1994	1995	1996	1997
Istanbul	4,074	3,563	4,727	5,757	5,959
Izmir	5,056	4,623	4,804	5,527	5,918
Mersin	11,667	10,874	11,714	11,587	13,189
Iskenderun	2,357	1,736	1,967	1,637	1,970
Derince	1,590	999	1,223	1,724	1,809
Bandirma	3,270	2,778	2,928	3,003	3,320
Samsun	1,824	1,215	1,870	2,408	2,563
TOTAL	**29,838**	**25,788**	**29,233**	**31,643**	**34,728**

Source: Turkish State Railways (1998).

Table 34
Specifications of the Port of Istanbul

Vessel type	Ship calls (vessels/year)	Berth length (m)	Max. depth (-m)	Loading/unloading capacity ('000 tons/year)
General cargo	1,134	1,784	10	3,035
Container	1,200	650	12	3,082
Dry bulk	79	190	10	
Ro-ro	238	141	8	
TOTAL	**2,651**	**2,765**	---	**6,117**

Source: Turkish State Railways (1998).

Table 35

General specifications of the ports of Turkish State Railways

Ports of Turkish State Railways	Berth length (m)	Port areas ('000m²)	Max. Draught (-m)	No. of workers	Total ship calls	Handling capacity ('000 tons/year)	Berth capacity ('000 tns/year)	Storage capacity General ('000 tons/year)	Contnrs
Istanbul	2,765	320	12	916	2,651	6,117	8,550	780	264
Izmir	2,959	902	14	564	3,640	6,564	11,100	944	324
Mersin	3,292	994	14.5	1,304	2,973	5,511	10,348	8,672	324
Iskenderun	1,426	750	12	664	640	3,224	6,097	9,286	146
Derince	1,472	312	15	299	1,105	3,452	4,101	3,152	15
Bandirma	2,788	246	12	294	4,280	3,008	7,008	2,013	15
Samsun	1,756	588	12	348	1,130	2,284	4,300	8,749	15
TOTAL	16,458	4,110	—	4,389	16,419	30,160	51,500	34,000	1,100

Source: Turkish State Railways: (1998).

Table 36

Total major cargoes handled at the Port of Istanbul between 1993 and 1997 ('000 tons)

Cargo type	1993	1994	1995	1996	1997
Dry bulk	25	68	42	32	81
General cargo	2,194	1,841	2,257	2,772	2,854
Container	1,855	1,654	2,428	2,953	3,024
TOTAL	**4,074**	**3,563**	**4,727**	**5,757**	**5,959**

Source: Turkish State Railways (1998)

Table 37

Cargo handling equipment of the Port of Istanbul

Cargo handling equipment	Unit	Capacity (tons)
Gantry crane	4	40
Shore and yard crane	20	3-25
Reach stacker	16	40
Transtainer	18	40
Mobile crane	18	5-25
Container forklift	22	10-42
General cargo forklift	68	2-5
Tugmaster	34	25
Loader	1	---
Electrical forklift	11	1.5
Trailer	71	20 and 40

Source: Turkish State Railways (1998)

The port, which is also known as the second major export and import gateway for the country after the Port of Istanbul, is also another exception to the typical port profile of Turkey in that it has an active container terminal. The port has a total berth length of 2,959 metres and has a vessel calling capacity of 3,640 vessels/year and a total cargo handling capacity of 6.564 million tons/year. The port is a well equipped modern container port with large storage areas and skilled personnel. Container vessels have a choice of seven berths of more than a length of 1,050 metres which can load and unload containers utilising four gantry cranes. The container terminal also includes reefer facilities allowing a continuous service for refrigerated containers. There is a special ro-ro and ferry berth and a passenger terminal with an annual berthing capacity of 238 ro-ro vessels. It will also be possible to service Panamax types of vessels following the completion of the dredging works in the Bay of Izmir. A specific container freight station is used for LCL containers. All variety of commodities are stored in warehouses and in open areas and secured by means of both control systems and port security services. Although a flexible and reliable service supply for 24 hours a day and 365 days a year is noted by the port management, 24 hours a day service actually cannot be accommodated because of the restrictions on the working hours of the customs office at the port, which is restricted to between 0800 and 1700 hours only.

Details of the port capacities of the Port of Izmir, the total of major cargoes handled between 1993 and 1997 and the cargo handling equipment of the port are illustrated in Tables 38, 39 and 40, respectively.

Table 38
Specifications of the Port of Izmir

Vessel type	Ship calls (vessels/year)	Berth length (m)	Max. depth (-m)	Loading/unloading capacity ('000 tons/year)
General cargo	810	1,429	10.5	1,666
Container	1,500	1,050	14	4,898
Dry bulk	79	150	10.5	-
Passenger	1,246	330	10.5	-
TOTAL	**3,635**	**2,959**	-	**6,564**

Source: Turkish State Railways (1998).

Table 39
Total major cargo handled at the Port of Izmir between 1993 and 1997 ('000 tons)

Cargo type	1993	1994	1995	1996	1997
Dry bulk	1,967	1,463	1,308	1,401	1,440
Liquid bulk	124	134	186	165	215
General cargo	1,006	595	543	629	557
Container	1,960	2,431	2,767	3,331	3,705
TOTAL	**5,057**	**4,623**	**4,804**	**5,526**	**5,917**

Source: Turkish State Railways (1998).

The management authority of the owner and operator of the Port of Izmir has adopted a new short term strategy to place and position this port as a hub port for the Eastern Mediterranean. Accordingly, cargo movements between the European Union and Izmir will be undertaken by larger vessels with feeder vessels distributing thereafter the cargo from Izmir to a number of smaller ports in this area, such as Pireaus in Greece, Port Said in Egypt and others in (for example) Syria or the Lebanon. In addition, a long term strategy of improved quality of service, better quality and improved equipment, reduced cargo damage and lower port prices was also adopted recently by the port authority (Interview, 1998).

Port of Mersin

In a similar fashion to the Ports of Istanbul and Izmir, the Port of Mersin is also one of Turkey's most important ports stemming in particular from its location on the Mediterranean Sea to the south of the country. In addition to

Table 40
Cargo handling equipment of the Port of Izmir

Cargo handling equipment	Unit	Capacity (tons)
Gantry crane	6	40
Shore and yard crane	9	3-25
Reach stacker	21	40
Transtainer	19	40
Mobile crane	14	5-25
Container forklift	28	10-42
General cargo forklift	47	2-5
Tugmaster	36	25
Loader	2	---
Electrical forklift	17	1.5
Trailer	62	20 and 40

Source: Turkish State Railways (1998).

cargo handling for foreign trades, considerable cargo is also transshipped between Europe and the Middle East and Mersin thus serves as a transit port for the region with oil as the major cargo type handled at the port. Cargo handling between 1993 and 1997 at the Port of Mersin is illustrated in Table 41.

Table 41
Total major cargoes handled at the Port of Mersin between 1993 and 1997 ('000 tons)

Cargo type	1993	1994	1995	1996	1997
Dry bulk	1,244	1,888	1,798	1,931	2,519
Liquid bulk	7,294	5,625	6,403	5,733	6,263
General cargo	1,878	2,010	1,905	1,919	1,557
Container	1,251	1,351	1,607	2,004	2,850
TOTAL	11,667	10,874	11,713	11,587	13,189

Source: Turkish State Railways (1998).

Major private ports

The major private ports amongst the 60 non state owned ports in Turkey are mostly situated on the Sea of Marmara to the northwest of the country. The most significant ones can be identified as the Ports of Gemport, Armaport, Kumport, Anatolian Cement Port, Mardas, Sedef, Colakoglu, Poliport and Bagfas in addition to a number of other, but less significant private ports. The ports of Kumport, Armaport, Anatolian Cement Port and Mardas are also known as the Ambarli Ports based upon their location in Ambarli in the Marmara region. The substructure, superstructure and highway connections at these private ports were constructed by their private owners and operators in general without subsidies or incentives provided by the state; however, there is an exception with the recently privatised Ports of Ordu, Giresun, Rize and Hopa, which were previously owned by the Turkish Maritime Organisation where some limited state aid was provided. A number of the specifications for these major private ports are given below in their respective sections.

Port of Gemport

The Port of Gemport was established in 1992 as the first private port in Turkey. The port is a general cargo port located in the Gulf of Gemlik and is connected to its hinterland by a good highway network. It has no rail connections. Berthing for ro-ro vessels is available through a combined terminal for car carriers. The port claims the highest efficiency for stuffing of containers, storage and distribution services. Cargo and container handling equipment used at the port has been improved based upon increasing total cargo handling capacity and an improved container handling system. Port facilities have also been developing rapidly through detailed consideration of local private sector port economics and at the same time, the rapid increases in the total number of customer shipping companies. ISO 9002 studies have also started for the port in an effort to formalise and to certify its rising quality amongst its competitors (Cargo News, 1998).

Operated by: Gemlik Port and Warehousing Administration Co.
Berths: Three berths with a total length of 435m and a maximum depth of 11m.
Maximum berthing: Eight vessels.
Cargo type: General cargo, container.
Equipment: Two mobile container cranes of 40 tons capacity
        One harbour crane of 26 tons capacity
        Two container handler stackers of 15 tons capacity.
        One ro-ro forklift of 35 tons capacity.
        One empty container stacker of 15 tons capacity.
        Ten forklift trucks of various capacity.
        Three terminal tractors.
Cargo handling capacity: 2,600,000 tons/year.
Capacity use: 85%.
Cargo storage area: 140,000 m^2 open and 2,000 m^2 closed areas, 5,000 TEU container stock capacity.
Foreign trade goods handled:
Imports: Steel roll, iron products, raw materials for textiles industry, automobile machinery parts, paper roll and iron scrap
Exports: Cotton yarn, textiles, tobacco, mining equipment and minerals, steel, pipes, ceramic products, foodstuff, fresh fruit and vegetables
Ship repair: Minor repairs.
Working hours : 24-hour service.

Port of Armaport

The port was established at the beginning of 1997, with a total investment value of US$ 1 billion, through a cooperation of shipowners with the aim of supplying the rapidly increasing demand for port services (International Transport News, 1998). Its internal infrastructure, and the connections of the port to the highway network were all constructed and built by private entrepreneurs. The Port of Armaport supplies the increasing needs of a range of dynamic services in the Marmara region with increasingly competitive prices and modern technological equipment in competition with the much higher port tariffs and the excessive container traffic that characterises Port Istanbul/Haydarpasa (The World, 1997). The port is positioned in a location as an alternative port to its main competitor, the Port of Istanbul which is located nearby and provides cargo handling services for both general liner and container shipping. An indicative comparison of price competition with its main competitor is given by a container unloading price of US$ 95 at the Port of Istanbul whilst the same service is only US$ 65 at the Port of Armaport. A major competitor for the port in international markets is the Port of Piraeus in Greece, which has developed into a hub port for the Russian Federation and other CIS countries, handling a total of 20,000 TEUs in transit shipments in 1997. Although the Port of Armaport aims to earn US$ 95 for each transit container handled at the port whilst the Port of Piraeus earns an estimated US$ 140 for a similar procedure, Armaport's prices remain more expensive compared with its Greek competitor because of the number and severity of government taxes which are imposed (The World, 1998c).

A ro-ro berth remains under construction to serve both ro-ro and lo-lo vessels in addition to the conventional container berths.

Operated by: Shipowners Port Management Co.

Berths: Four berths with a total length of 569m and a maximum depth of 12m.

Maximum berthing: up to 50,000 dwt vessels.

Cargo type: General cargo, container.

Equipment: Four mobile container cranes of 80, 63, 30 and 20 tons capacity.

Three container stackers of 45 tons capacity.

One container stacker of 18 tons capacity.

Three forklifts of various capacity.

Two terminal tractors of 40 tons capacity.

Two loaders.

Four bunkers.

One conveyor.

Two weighbridges of 100 tons capacity.

Cargo handling capacity: 1,000,000 tons/year; 50,000 TEUs.

Capacity use: 65%.

Cargo storage area: 60,000 m^2 open and 5,000 m^2 closed areas; 50,000 m^2 container stock capacity.

Fire fighting: available.

Working hours : 24 hours/day, 365 days/year.

Port of Kumport

The port of Kumport is situated to the north of the Sea of Marmara with its own multipurpose terminal. The port is operated by the Association of Sea Sanders in Istanbul. The container terminal of the port is operated by a group formed by Kumport Port Management and Arkas Shipping Group - one of the leading Izmir based group of shipping companies dealing in freight forwarding, logistics, shipowning and ship operating areas of the shipping industry (Cargo News, 1998).

Operated by: Kumport Port Management Co.
Berths: Four berths with a total length of 640m and a maximum depth of 20m.
Cargo type: All cargo except liquid bulk.
Cargo storage area: 80,000 m^2
Pilotage: Compulsory, provided by Turkish Maritime Organisation.
Working hours: 24 hours/day, 365 days/year.

Port of Mardas

Operated by: Mardas Marmara Ship Management Co.
Berths: Total length of 800m and ro-ro berthing with a maximum depth of 14.5m.
Maximum berthing: up to 178,000 dwt.
Cargo type: Scrapping, ferroalloys, pig-iron, rebars, pipe, paper, wood, coal, sugar, palletised cargo, dry and liquid bulk, containers.
Equipment: Mobile container cranes of 20 tons capacity.
                  Two scrap handlers.
                  Four grapples each of 45m^3 and 8m^3 capacities.
                  Two generators one each of 380 kVA and 850 kVA.
                  Magnetic sweeper.
                  Loader.
                  Two weighbridges of 100 tons capacity.
Cargo storage area: 40,000 m^2 open area.
Fire fighting: available.
Working hours : 24 hours/day, 365 days/year.

Port of Sedef Container Terminal

Operated by: Sedef Ship Industry Co.
Berths: Total length of 457m and ro-ro and lo-lo berthing with a maximum depth of 15m.
Cargo type: Conventional cargo, containers
Equipment: Four mobile cranes of 110, 85, 50 and 30 tons capacity. One of 40 tons, three of 25 tons, one of 20 tons, one of 14 tons and three of 10 tons.
Top lifter of 44 tons capacity.
Side lifter of eight tons capacity.
Forklifts - one of seven tons and three of three tons capacity.
Terminal tractor.
Cargo storage area: 52,750 m^2 open area, 3,000 TEU storage capacity.
Working hours : between 0830 - 2200 hours, 365 days/year.

Port of Colakoglu

Operated by: Colakoglu Metallurgy Co.
Berths: Total length of 680m with a maximum depth of 13m.
Cargo type: Iron and steel products.
Equipment: Cranes of various capacity; magnetic grabs.
Cargo handling capacity: 1,000 - 3,000 m/day of steel and iron products.
Working hours : 24 hours/day, 365 days/year.

Port of Giresun

The Port of Giresun - formerly owned and operated by the Turkish Maritime Organisation and situated on the Black Sea, was recently leased for 30 years and is currently operated by the Giresun Port Management Company of the Cakiroglu Building and Construction Company. The port management company employs 26 personnel a reduction from a total of 140 people in former times. Timber, leather, flour, wheat and a number of agricultural products are the main cargo types handled at the port in foreign trade between Turkey and the CIS countries. The port management group aims to position the port to gain an increase in the share of sea transport against land transport for exports of hazelnuts - the most distinctive export product in Giresun.

Container handling has also been developing at the port and a 60-ton-capacity mobile crane and a forklift are on the list of items to be purchased for the port. An additional quay will be implemented using a filled area to provide a considerably improved and expanded container terminal.

Port of Rize

The Port of Rize is one the former Turkish Maritime Organisation ports, and is currently operated by Rize Port Management and Investment Company established by three shipping groups of companies - the Yerdimci, Ergencler and Cillioglu Groups. The investment project for the port envisages developments in the long-term according to the demand either for passenger shipping or industrial trading based upon the free zone that already exists at the port.

The port is the terminal for ferry services between Rize, the Russian Federation and the CIS countries in the Black Sea area and has a recently refurbished passenger terminal. The port management also plans to position the port as one of the developing container terminals for liner shipping in the region.

Port of Hopa

The Port of Hopa, similar to the Ports of Giresun and Rize, is one of the former Turkish Maritime Organisation ports and is a recently privatised port situated at the far eastern end of the Black Sea Region on the north coast of Turkey and located very close to the border with Georgia. The port was leased to Park Shipping and Hopa Port Management Company for 30 years in 1997 and is currently operated by this company (Chamber of Shipping, 1998c). The port management aims to become a competitor of the Port of Poti in the CIS countries by placing itself as an export and import gateway to and from the Russian Federation and the CIS countries and providing improved, more efficient and faster port services compared to its competitors in the region. In addition, another goal of the port management is to reposition the port as the first step on the "silk road" of ancient times by concentrating upon imports of oil, cotton, minerals and iron from the Turkish Republics in Central Asia and exports of food stuffs, textiles and construction materials to these countries.

Heavy investments were made in the port by the managing company aimed at enlarging the facilities to 25,000 m^2 of concrete area, and the closed area of

2,000 m^2 to 18,000 m^2, where 18,000 tons of cotton could be stored and also the warehousing area of 7,000 m^2 to 77,000 m^2 of which 25,000 m^2 will be reserved as a container storage area. Obsolete forklift trucks were replaced with five new ones and container handling cranes together with a 40-ton-capacity mobile crane were purchased to operate in the port. On the other hand, the port management group have been complaining about the absence of a free zone at the port, which could have been developed because the Port of Hopa is the biggest port in the region and is a border-crossing focal point for coastal trading between Turkey and Georgia.

Conclusions

This review of the ports sector in Turkey has provided the background to the ship operating and owning sections which were covered earlier. The two sectors are clearly highly interrelated even though a large proportion of shipping activity occurs outside ports and in other international locations.

We will now move on to the other parts of the maritime sector, beginning with the ancillary industries, followed by a discussion of the shipbuilding, repair and scrapping industries before moving on to assess policies for the Turkish maritime sector as a whole and the shipping industry in particular.

5. The ancillary industries and sectors

Introduction

In addition to the major indicators and issues and the current situation of the shipping and ports industry in Turkey, a number of activities in the ancillary maritime industries are also explained briefly in this section. Freight forwarding, agency services, shipbroking, insurance, customs services, finance and banking services are the major examples of supporting ancillary industries for the maritime industry that are discussed here.

Freight forwarding, agency services and shipbroking

Development of foreign trade has led to a globalisation in world economies, which has directly affected the maritime sector through an increase in cargo movements and significant development of intermodal transportation and thus the role of freight forwarding. *Freight forwarders* - formerly commonly the cargo carriers - have also developed and reconstructed their activities by now dealing with the organisation of the transport system from the beginning of production to the final point of consumption of the product where it reaches the consumer. As a result of the reconstruction of the role of transportation and the widening of the focus for freight forwarding, the responsibilities of a number of jobs e.g. carrier, shipper, forwarder etc. now require closer attention.

The Association of Freight Forwarders and Transporters - UTIKAD - was recently established in Turkey and has a total of 112 members at present. The association is an equivalent of FIATA and focuses upon all modes of transport as well as international transport, combined transport and logistics. In addition, it serves the needs of freight forwarders and foreign traders by issuing a number of certificates, including the FBL - FIATA Bill of Lading and FCR - Forwarders Certificate of Receipt, which are approved by the ICC - International Chamber of Commerce (The World, 1998b).

Some of the major problems that are faced by freight forwarders in Turkey, who are also dealing with land transport in certain areas, have stemmed mainly from services to, from and through the CIS countries, caused by for example, a 200% price increase in road passes, insecurity of the highway network in the Russian Federation and the Balkans in such countries as Romania and Bulgaria, restrictions upon visas for entry into some countries, and limitations placed upon total cargo tonnages for Bulgaria, Greece, Romania, the Ukraine, the Russian Federation and Iran (International Transport News, 1998).

A *shipping agency* is the agent of a shipowner or a charterer, who deals with practical shipping services such as berthing, loading and unloading of cargo and ship supplies at the port, to and from which the cargo is shipped. An agent is the representative of the shipowner or the charterer and serves the needs of that shipowner or ship charterer. Most of the shipping agencies in Turkey have served as freight forwarders in the industry for a very many years. Since freight forwarding has been developing considerably in recent years, the services of both agencies and freight forwarders have tended to be processed through the same companies unlike the situation in the ancillary sector in many established shipping countries.

Shipbroking mainly deals with fixing a charter party between a shipper and a carrier, which are the operator and shipowner in some cases or charterer's charterer and shipowner's charterer in some others. A shipbroker's duty is to bring together the purchaser and seller to sign the agreement. In practice, a shipbroker's duties - as a middleman - may vary from the activities of shipping and chartering to services related to the purchasing and selling of a ship.

The duties of shipping agents in Turkey vary from case to case and from company to company. Whilst one agent may only deal with documentation at the port, another agent may act as a freight forwarder by also having responsibilities for the cargo. In some cases in the Turkish shipping industry, a shipping agent also acts as a shipbroker by providing chartering services for a shipowner. Since these supporting and ancillary industries have not been fully established yet and are still developing within the shipping industry in Turkey, the duties of shipping agents, freight forwarders and shipbrokers remain commonly mixed together although they are most commonly provided through shipping agents.

Insurance and law

Since freight forwarding has only a recently become a rapidly developing area of support to the shipping industry, a number of serious problems require solutions to be resolved through the development and application of a series of maritime laws, by-laws and regulations some of which were indicated and discussed under the legal context in Chapter Two. The role of insurance in freight forwarding and in shipping in particular, plays a crucial role in helping to resolve some of the problems in the context of legal problems. A large number of existing and increasing problems have been observed by insurance companies and they have been developing their activities in Turkey as a consequence. The widespread use of insurance policies has started to be adopted for freight transport of all sorts and these policies have been based upon a series of new regulations and laws, recently prepared and designed by the Turkish Ministry of Transport. This includes the Law of Cargo Carrying, in particular (International Transport News, 1998). Since most shipping agencies in Turkey play the role of freight forwarders as well, the job titles and responsibilities of freight forwarders will need to be defined within the legal context of this and other relevant laws by the Turkish Parliament. Insurance policies differ from one type of good to another, and consequently, their precise definition is needed to make the enforcement of these regulations practical. Much of this regulation remains to be carried out.

Insurance services have not fully developed yet within the transport sector in Turkey, and in the shipping industry in particular. As a consequence, some very rapid action is needed in this dynamic industry in the context of accelerating developments in foreign trade. Many shipping companies have neglected insurance services either because of their own irresponsibility or because of the unwillingness of a number of insurance companies to take on the risk of an undefined nature for certain types of cargo (International Transport News, 1998).

Customs services

In addition to customs services provided directly by the Customs Officials at formal customs locations, a number of independent Turkish companies have started operating their own systems recently within the foreign trade sector in an attempt to save time in completing paperwork and to simplify the heavy bureaucracy at customs offices at seaports and airports that tends to exist. These companies are currently developing rapidly in Turkey with some of them establishing their own computerised customs systems.

Customs law and regulations have been the main points of reference for these companies. In addition to complying with the requirements of these laws and regulations, companies providing customs services have also been dealing with processing customs papers, tax papers and subsidy papers and tracking the status of goods at customs. Issues such as invoicing customers have become easier by the recent development of specific computer software programmes and on-line system between customers and foreign traders, and the customs service providers.

One of the leading customs service providers in Turkey - Solmaz Customs Services - has recently started interactive electronic customs services by placing a number of forms for customs activities, costing and other related procedures on a web page on the internet system to be filled in by foreign trading organisations (International Transport News, 1998). Customs Tariff Statistical Position Numbers for each type of merchandise have been listed on their web page, otherwise known as "the Blue Book of Turkish Customs System", so that those involved in foreign trading are able to find the total amount of tax to be paid at customs offices, the name of the institution from which to gain permission for foreign trading and the specific conditions that exist at customs offices for both imports and exports. The company is now the leading one in the industry providing facilities for export permissions for merchandise, customs services, domestic transport and packaging, international transport (in conjunction with the appropriate freight forwarder), paperwork for subsidy approval where applicable or the provision of incentives to customs services in the country of purchase.

Finance, banking and leasing in the maritime sector

Costs, financial sourcing and finding resources to match costs and investments are crucial issues for all companies. The costing items that are appropriate for one set of companies differs from those appropriate for another. A number of costs in shipping companies are listed in Table 42 which is indicative of the complexity of the issue within the shipping sector and consequently the need for a strong and supportive financial sector to provide adequate and appropriate support.

Finance in shipping companies is different from finance in other industries because of the nature of the business which is considerably dictated by the need for very high investment and capital values. The capital of many companies dealing in most industries other then shipping can be expressed as:

initial capital + increases of capital + undistributed profits - losses

in other words, capital is made up of total assets less the losses on the balance sheet and, therefore, the capital of that company can become a security element in the case of financing any losses. However in the shipping business, the capital of a company in terms of cash flows is commonly insufficient either for investments or to match losses in the shipping business particularly because of the high values of ships. Therefore, there is little option other than for shipping investments to be financed either by receiving loans or borrowing money from financial sources. Approximately 80% of investment in the shipping industry is received from banking credits or loans and the remaining 20% is matched by the capital of the companies concerned. Therefore, the ratio of debt to capital is approximately 4:1 in the shipping industry whilst the same ratio is approximately 1:1 in many other industries (Caki, 1996). This situation is certainly the case in Turkey.

Financial sources for shipping in Turkey other than the capital of the company in the maritime sector consist of bank loans and shipyard credits and loans in particular, with minor credits received from public capital, public debts and private sector debts. Banks have not supported investments in shipping in terms of credits or loans because of the relatively unstable economy in Turkey. Therefore, common with many other countries in this position, the need for banks specialised in the maritime sector has arisen in Turkey. Denizbank - The Maritime Bank - was established as a specialist state owned bank serving mostly the maritime sector; however, it was transferred to Emlakbank - a state owned bank specialised in housing and mortgages - at the beginning of the 1990s. As a result, additional banking services are needed for the maritime sector, and therefore, an urgent need exists for a new specialist bank to be developed. In addition to Emlakbank, the VakifDeniz (Foundation-Sea) Leasing Company which is effectively part of another bank - Vakifbank - is active in dealing in the financial leasing of ships but remains non specialist in nature.

Table 42
Indicative costs in the shipping sector

Initial materials and material costs.	Labour wages and expenditure.
Social expenditure.	Loading and unloading expenditure.
Cargo shifting.	Additional working hour wages.
Officer wages and expenditure.	Seamens' wages.
Spare seamens' wages.	Other benefits and services.
Pointer costs.	Transmitting costs.
Vessel shifting.	Waiting cost of ship.
Stuffing material costs.	Pilotage costs.
Tug costs.	Service pipe costs.
Port costs.	Berth costs.
Agency costs and commissions.	Freight forwarder commissions.
Freight discounts.	Shipbroking.
Transport expenditure.	Maintenance and repair expenditures of vessels.
Shipchandling expenditure.	Miscellaneous expenditure.
Advertising expenditure.	Notary expenditure.
Survey expenditure.	Dispatch expenditure.
Tax and official expenditure.	Depreciation.
Vessel depreciation.	Vessel inventory depreciation.
Vessel insurance expenditure.	Financial expenditure.
Seamens' additional costs.	

e.g. emergency premiums. additional working hour wages.
Heating, cooling, lighting, fresh water and cleaning expenditure.
Disinfection expenditure.

Source: Caki, 1996.

Shipyard credits and loans are the other main financial sources received by companies in the maritime sector. Since shipbuilding is a long term and a high-cost activity, these types of financial sources are not commonly preferred mostly because of the payback conditions of the loan for the sector. For example, a loan received for the building of a ro-ro vessel amounting to 25% of the total investment will commonly be required to be paid back over ten years with a very high annual interest rate of 50%. Some support that does exist for shipbuilding worldwide are state subsidies, credits, incentives for exports, research and development, warranty exemption, V.A.T. exemption, customs tax exemption and some low-cost and long-term credits and they are received by shipyards in a number of countries, such as Japan, Korea, France, Germany, the Netherlands and Norway whilst only loans and credits for shipbuilding and exports of ships are available in Turkey (Caki, 1996; The Secretariat of Transportation, 1996). A comparison of some subsidies and incentives received by companies in the maritime sector in the European Union and Turkey are listed in Table 43. Also apparent from the same table is that both the state subsidies and incentives received in Turkey are very limited compared to the ones available in the European Union.

Financial problems arising from insufficient loans, credits and incentives in the maritime sector are currently considered problems in Turkey for the maritime sector that await consideration. The result has been that shipping entrepreneurs have tended to attempt to solve their own financial problems carrying their own risks either by receiving loans from foreign banks or renting and purchasing vessels through financial leasing (The World, 1997).

Leasing in the maritime sector

Leasing has recently been used in the maritime sector and has been a rapidly increasing method for financial sources in the sector since the middle of the 1990s. Thousands of US$ are paid for insurance premiums for high-value ships. Financial leasing has been an advantageous method in the sector for ship operating companies that are currently collaborating with leasing companies in purchasing and operating ships. In addition to its advantages for the maritime sector, the method is also considered advantageous in finding financial sources for other sectors in the export and import business. Financial leasing in the maritime sector has a share of 21% of the total amount of leasing that is undertaken in Turkey with an approximate annual increase in the 1990s of 52% whilst the total amount of financial leasing in the country continues to increase at a rate of 31% annually (The Economist, 1995). For example, funds to a total amount of US$ 180 million were made available by VakifDeniz Leasing Company for leasing ships between 1993 and 1997 providing leading financial support in the mid-term period (The World, 1997).

Advantages of financial leasing in the maritime sector are:

100% finance in investments of ships compared to partial investments by bank loans and credits.
Leasing does not affect operating capital and the credibility of a company.
Flexibility in payments, i.e. planned payments based upon cash flow and revenues of a company.
Financial liquidity for a company, i.e. a shipowner may sell a ship to a financial leasing company and lease the same ship so that he can use that money.
Exemption from tax.
Low VAT.

Leasing payments can be simplified by incentives in the investment of ships.
Less bureaucracy compared to bank loans and credits (Caki, 1996).

Table 43

A comparison of subsidies and incentives received by maritime companies in the European Union and Turkey

Type of subsidy/incentive	EU	Turkey
A. Subsidy for capital	Applied in terms of development level of the region of a country, where the investment is made.	No subsidy.
B. Subsidy for interest rates	A specific percentage of capital investments, which could be delayed for a limited period of time, and differs according to the development level of a region.	No subsidy.
C. Incentives for taxes	VAT discount. Tax discounts for specific items differing according to the development level of a region. Tax discounts for equipment.	Customs tax discounts. Investment discounts. Financial fund discounts.
D. Credits	A number of credits differing according to the development level of a region.	Credit - 25% of the total shipbuilding value, borrowed from Turkish Development Bank for shipbuilding and paid back in five years.

Source: Development Centre for the Economy - IGEME (1995).

Although the total tonnage of the Turkish merchant fleet keeps increasing year by year, unfortunately the share of cargo carrying by vessels operating under foreign flags has also been increasing and therefore, the total amount of freight rate payments in terms of foreign exchange continues to rise resulting in a disadvantageous situation both for Turkish shipping and the Turkish economy. As a result of this, financial leasing as the major financial source for investment in shipping, in purchasing ships or newbuildings, in particular has become a crucial element and will be required to be used more and more in the future to solve many of the financial problems that face the Turkish shipping industry.

Conclusions

This chapter has attempted to give a brief outline of the maritime ancillary sector in Turkey and thus to paint a background to the mainstream shipping activities in which we have most interest. Turkey displays an immature level of development in this sector despite its growing and sizeable ports and shipping interests. However, with time, activities particularly in the broking agency and forwarding areas are likely to grow. Further maturity in the legal and financial sides will come with time but is likely to remain dominated by the financial and legal organisations already existing in the west.

6. The shipbuilding, ship repair and scrapping industries in Turkey

The shipbuilding industry

A ship is constructed by bringing together a substantial number of components and a considerable amount of equipment to the appropriate shipyard, and by producing various parts of the ship within that shipyard eventually to form the body of the ship, in accordance with the detailed plan for the project. This involves gathering together at the shipyards, products from a wide variety of industrial sectors, such as output from the iron and steel industry, engineering sector, paints, many products made of wood and plastics, advanced electronics products etc. The ship is the output from the shipbuilding industry and therefore, this industry forms a major substructure for the maritime sector as a whole. Its significance is therefore, hard to over-emphasise.

The shipbuilding industry thus forms a significant part of the maritime sector, and has close relations with the wider manufacturing and assembling industry. This industry has the potential to earn considerable foreign exchange, encourages the development of auxiliary industries, attracts the transfer of technology, provides sizeable opportunities for employment, supports the national merchant fleet and contributes significantly to the needs of national defence. Therefore, its contribution to the maritime sector as well as to the national economy is widely considered important in many countries including Turkey.

This section of the book concentrates upon the development of the shipbuilding industry in Turkey, its place within the Turkish maritime sector and in particular, the place of private shipyards in the industry. The shipbuilding industry has really developed in Turkey only since the beginning of the 1960s but since then has been one of the most significant industries in the country throughout the 1970s and the 1980s.

We have seen earlier how the maritime sector has been a rapidly growing and developing sector in Turkey incorporating a large range of activities such as the shipping industry, shipbuilding industry, the ship scrapping industry, the yachting industry, the marina sector, a wide variety of ancillary industries etc. However, the shipbuilding industry has been one of the major industries of the Turkish maritime sector measured in particular in terms of its direct contribution to the national economy. This industry, covering as it does newbuildings, restorations, alterations, dry docking, assembling, repairing and maintenance procedures for all types of floating vehicle, has a crucially important role deriving from Turkey's ageing merchant fleet and its pressing need for revitalisation in particular. In addition, the shipbuilding industry is dependent upon various productions of steel construction and shipbuilding secondary industries thus increasing its industrial significance (Nehir, 1993).

The development of the Turkish shipbuilding industry

During the period between 1950 and 1963, the Turkish shipbuilding industry, which was then limited to the construction of small vessels, barges, buoys, various mooring boats and tug boats, started to build larger vessels. Examples of this new trend included a number of 6,500 dwt general cargo ships, a series of ferries, and various tug boats and passenger ships. In 1962, this growth in output was characterised by the construction of a floating dock with 10,000-15,000 tonne lifting capacity (Chamber of Naval Architects, 1989). The period following 1963 is known as the Period of the Planned Economy in Turkey because of the existence and implementation of a series of Five-Year Development Plans by the Turkish Government. The first significant steps that were taken for the Turkish shipbuilding industry occurred during this planned period.

Starting from 1963, the development of the maritime industry in general, took place in parallel with the development of the economy as a whole.

During the First Five-Year Development Plan, between the years 1963 to 1967, the main target for the shipbuilding industry was for the shipyards in Turkey to concentrate upon meeting the domestic demand for ships. The Turkish shipyards were technically quite capable of supplying all of the domestic demands and constructing all the types of needed vessels. With respect to the needs of the economy of the country, imports of all ships were reduced as a result between 1963 and 1965. A variety of vehicle ferries, passenger ferries and a number of merchant ships were constructed in Turkish shipyards.

After 1965, the demand for ships filled Turkish shipyards so that capacity was achieved. These economically brave decisions were an important step in the expansion of the shipbuilding industry and as a result of that, the public sector shipyards developed considerably along with the development of some private sector shipyards. A respected credit mechanism had been developed during this time and a significant amount of credit was supplied during this period. During the same period, there arose the need for a substantial investment in order to bring the significant Camialti shipyard up to a standard to build modern ships. This shipyard had facilities that would enable the construction of vessels up to 20,000 dwt along with modern workshops which were completed in 1970.

During the Second Five-Year Development Plan between 1968 and 1972, economic precautions were taken so that the shipbuilding capacity in the country could be increased and modernised. It was a major principle in undertaking this investment that the demand for ships had to be met from domestic resources. However, for the sole purpose of quickly enlarging the fleet and provided that it did not damage the domestic shipbuilding industry, dry cargo vessels, large tankers and special types of other vessels could be imported. Limited imports were also permitted because domestic ship demands could not be met by the existing shipyards because of both overlarge ship dimensions and constraints upon the annual production quotas. The Pendik shipyard, which was originally planned for construction in 1939, was finally included in the 1969 investment plan. In 1974, the banks begun again to make credit investments to support ship building contracts and to provide financial support for the purchase of foreign supplies. In particular in this case, the finance for the dry dock amounted to a significant value and all the other works other than the dry dock had been completed. It was decided to build half a dry dock and a slipway to enable the building of ships up to 60,000 dwt. The slipway was finally completed in 1982.

Amongst the target actions included in the Third Five-Year Development Plan between 1973 and 1977, was the setting of a target that the necessary systems and organisations would be established to provide for and facilitate the Merchant Marine Fleet offering services to foreign markets. One of the purposes of having an effective Merchant Marine Fleet, is to prevent paying high cargo prices caused by foreign dependence and to gain increased competitive power in foreign markets. As a consequence and similar to previous plans, it was also a target for the shipbuilding industry to supply domestic demands and to be developed as a source of exports. With these considerations, and in addition to the Pendik yard investment, the project of improving the Alaybey yard to a reasonable status as a repair yard in the Aegean region was included in the investment programme.

It was planned for 1975 that the Turkish Merchant Marine Fleet and the shipbuilding industry were both to be developed as part of a structured social and economic programme and that this would run in partnership with the planned replacement of the national defence network. Additionally, another planned target was that the Turkish Merchant Marine Fleet was to be expanded to a level so that it could supply around 50% of the Turkish foreign trade transportation needs rapidly, safely and economically. Any vessel needs which could not be supplied from domestic production for whatever reason would be imported (Chamber of Naval Architects, 1989). During the same period, the capacity of all the shipyards was substantially increased, and as a result the demand for vessels could be met almost entirely from domestic resources. As a consequence, only very large ships, large tankers and specialist types of ship demands had to be fulfilled by imports.

During the period of the Fourth Five-Year Development Plan between 1979 and 1983, the shipbuilding areas in Tuzla in the Marmara region, were widely scattered amongst a large number of shipbuilders and so it was planned to gather together the shipbuilding industry in the Tuzla area to act as a competitor to the shipyards that were located in Istanbul in this region. As a result of these improvements, between 1981 and 1983, a total of 89 ships grossing 220,000 dwt was constructed consisting of a range of vessels between 1,500 and 75,000 dwt at the shipyards operated by companies from the private sector alone. However, after 1985 shipbuilding in the private sector shipyards ceased completely and the entire shipbuilding industry, but especially that of the private sector, fell into economic crisis. This crisis continued until 1987.

In 1988, the Central Bank of Turkey postponed the credit debts of the Marine Bank and as a result, the bank started to make repayment agreements with the shipbuilders, so that the financial obstruction that had caused the problems in the industry was cleared. In more recent years, as a result of continued efforts within the shipbuilding industry to open up to foreign countries, one of the private sector shipyards has been successful in attracting an order for 24 x 4,200 dwt ships, and another has orders to build a series of steel barges for a Dutch company. Many others in the private sector have negotiated orders with foreign firms. Turkish shipbuilding prices are approximately 20% cheaper than many other countries in spite of the drawbacks of relative technological inefficiency and the longer construction time period that normally occurs. This financial advantage needs to be built upon in order to open the market to a larger number of foreign countries.

With the separation of the shipyards from the Marine Bank and the establishment of the General Directorate of the Turkish Ship Industry Company, the state owned shipyards are now operated by the Turkish Ship Industry Company. The largest ships that have been able to be built in the country have been the two 75,000 dwt bulk ships for the Turkish Maritime Organisation and they were designed and constructed at Pendik shipyard. The engines - Pendik-Sulzer (A Type) - were produced under a Sulzer licence, can generate up to 35,000 BHP and have been used elsewhere as the main engines on relatively smaller ships and as the generators on larger ships running with diesel oil.

Regarding the report on the shipbuilding industry of the Sixth Five-Year Development Plan for the Turkish economy, the target for total tonnage was determined after consideration of the import and export predictions for the country. As a consequence, a projection for newbuildings by Turkish shipyards has been made for the period between 1989 and 1994. The total tonnage of the Turkish merchant fleet was targeted to reach 6.5 million dwt which includes approximately 1.5 million dwt of newbuildings. However, domestic newbuildings were considerably less than the planned quantities.

Turkish shipbuilding industry in the world

Almost 90% of the world trade by volume is transported by sea and the demand for sea transport keeps increasing parallel to the development of world trade. Ships that are the instruments of sea transport have only a limited useful period of productivity from the point of view of their technical and economic characteristics. Under heavy working conditions and the corrosive effects of sea water, ships rapidly deteriorate and their maintenance and repair costs increase as they age, and as a result they lose their economic efficiency. In combination with this process of predictable decay, shipowners dispose of their vessels and renew their fleet when freight rates become more profitable, and this leads to increased demand for new shipbuildings. Moreover, as a result of the extending range of the uses of intermodal transport and changes in world trade, new types of vessels have started to be built which incorporate a substantial degree of high technology. The increasing productivity of these newly designed vessels has affected the demand for newbuildings which has increased notably.

Similar to shipbuilding industries in many countries in the world, the Turkish shipbuilding industry was also directly affected by uncertainty in market conditions. It was badly affected by the crisis in world sea transport during the mid 1980s in particular, which caused a decline in vessel prices. In addition, the imbalanced national economy led to decreases in subsidies for shipowners and shipbuilders in Turkey.

Output from Turkish shipyards was 68,000 grt annually by the late 1980s representing some 2% of the total West European merchant ship output. This turnaround in fortune from the mid 1980s depression, was achieved as a consequence of the injection of massive amounts of state funds and substantial orders largely from both German and Polish shipowners. New orders in the shipbuilding industry for the first five countries in the world and Turkey at the end of 1996 are illustrated in Table 44. As can be seen from the table, Turkey was the 16th country in the world with total new orders of 48 vessels amounting to 539,294 dwt. The total of new orders in the world was 74,923,435 dwt at the end of 1996 (Chamber of Shipping, 1997).

In addition to the information provided in the table, Turkish shipbuilding output and new orders compared to world shipbuilding output and new orders in 1996 were as follows:

  5 tankers out of a total of 192;
  2 bulkers out of a total of 2,152;
  4 container vessels out of a total of 125;
  17 general cargo vessels out of a total of 196;
  6 passenger ships/ferries out of a total of 132.

Furthermore, Turkish shipbuilding output and new orders compared to the world figures in gross tonnages are as follows:

  164,000 grt of tankers out of a total of 8,742,000 grt;
  84,000 grt of bulkers out of a total of 7,185,000 grt;
  15,000 grt of container vessels out of a total of 3,493,000 grt;
  106,000 grt of general cargo vessels out of a total of 1,274,000 grt;
  9,000 grt of passenger ships/ferries out of a total of 2,358,000 grt.

The current situation in the Turkish shipbuilding industry

The current total output capacity of Turkish shipyards is approximately 500,000 dwt/year for newbuildings and six million dwt/year for ship repairs.

However, the average actual usage of the capacity of all shipyards is somewhere between 10 and 20%, which is generally considered to be a low figure for the country. Since there are strong links and a high interdependence between the primary shipbuilding industry and the secondary shipbuilding supply industry, total employment for the sector is not limited to the primary shipbuilding industry alone. It is estimated that one person employed in the primary shipbuilding industry provides employment for three more people in the secondary shipbuilding industry in Turkey.

Table 44
Shipbuilding orders in Turkey and in the world (31.12.1996)

Ranking	Country	Total number of vessels	Total tonnage of new orders (dwt)
1.	Japan	596	26,334,644
2.	South Korea	322	22,981,139
3.	People's Rep. of China	228	6,029,073
4.	Poland	125	3,365,795
5.	Germany	130	2,291,630
16.	**Turkey**	**48**	**539,294**
	The world		**74,923,435**

Source: Chamber of Shipping, 1997.

Technical capacity and conditions

Wooden, steel, aluminium and fibreglass vessels have all been constructed in Turkish shipyards. The largest number of enterprises which fabricate steel, aluminium, wooden and fibreglass ships are gathered together in Istanbul and in the Marmara region but there are some units in Karadeniz Ereglisi, Izmir and Tatvan. Generally wooden shipbuilding has been located in the Black Sea region (Trabzon, Zonguldak) in Marmara (Tuzla, Sariyer, Kucukcekmece, Selimpasa) in the Aegean region (Izmir, Fethiye) and in the Mediterranean region (Bodrum, Marmaris, Alanya). Fibreglass vessel production is carried on in Istanbul and Izmir. Wooden and fibreglass constructions are used for smaller vessels and yachts, mainly for leisure purposes that play an important role in the Turkish tourism sector. Steel and aluminium shipbuilding institutions are located in Istanbul and in the Marmara region and there are also units in Karadeniz Ereglisi, Izmir and Tatvan.

There has arisen a notable need to upgrade the shipbuilding industry in Turkey caused by the rapid growth of the shipping industry. This need has been exacerbated by the ageing facilities and technology of these shipyards in particular in comparison with the shipyards in developed countries. Therefore, a number of steps have been taken to improve productivity and to establish advantageous arrangements for financial development. Furthermore, a consortium of Turkish shipowners has made plans to import Japanese shipbuilding technology and other improvements for shipyards together with a sizeable loan from Japan (Drewry, 1995).

The economic situation

The contribution of the current total capacity of the shipbuilding industry to the Turkish economy can be summarised as follows:

> Net shipbuilding capacity: approximately 500,000 dwt per year.
> Added value to the current capacity: US$ 1.2 billion per year.
> Added value of the current capacity in terms of net exchange rate inputs: US$ 600 million per year.
> Added value of the current capacity to employment (including the secondary shipbuilding industry): 105 million man-hours per year.
> Revenue to the Turkish economy regarding the usage of current total capacity (including taxes, insurance, funds, interest rates, etc.): US$ 340 million per year.
> Rate of domestic added value: 40%.
> (Interview, 1998b).

There are various targets for the development of the Turkish shipbuilding industry. It is known that if the current capacity of the Turkish shipyards are increased through technical improvements, then the economic situation of the industry will also be improved. Therefore, the following moves have also been planned by State Planning Organisation for the Turkish shipbuilding industry within the Seventh Five-Year Development Plan for the period between 1995 and 1999:

> New shipbuilding capacity: 1,000,000 dwt/year.
> Ship repair capacity: 7,500,000 dwt/year.
> Added value of the shipbuilding industry to the economy: US$ 1.5 billion per year.

Added value of the total capacity to employment (including the secondary shipbuilding industry): 125 million man-hours per year.
Rate of domestic added value: 65%.
(Chamber of Shipping, 1995a).

The following developments are recommended within the Seventh Five-Year Development Plan to help achieve the above targets during the period between 1995 and 1999:

Support in the form of extended maritime education and training with respect to shipyards.
New shipbuilding projects and increased marketing of these and other projects.
Improving the substructures of shipyards.
New subsidies.
Privatisation of state owned shipyards.
Establishment of a specialised sector bank.

The financial situation

Regarding the Seventh Five-Year Development Plan which is in effect between 1995 and 1999, the total capacity of the Turkish merchant fleet is estimated and planned to reach approximately 20 million dwt from a figure which was 10.56 million dwt at the end of 1997. This total amount is estimated to reach 15 million dwt during the middle of this planned period. Furthermore, this means that an average of 1.5 million dwt of ships is expected to join the Turkish merchant fleet each year during this planned period. If between 10 and 15% of the new members of the fleet are estimated to be newbuildings, then approximately 150,000 dwt of newbuildings are planned for each year during this period. In addition, the required finance for the building of a new ship is estimated at around US$ 1,000 per dwt (UNCTAD, 1994). Therefore, the total annual financial requirement of newbuildings of the Turkish shipbuilding industry during the planned period between 1995 and 1999 amounts to approximately US$ 150 million.

Subsidies and loans

The total utilisation capacity within the shipbuilding industry in the world has declined following the freight crisis and the decrease in the availability of loans after 1985. The Turkish shipbuilding industry was also markedly affected by this crisis. True and effective competition between the shipyards in Turkey and those in the rest of the world was far beyond the capability of the Turkish shipyards. Subsidies to the industry from the Turkish Government are compared with those in the rest of the world in Table 45.

Long term loans by the Government for the shipbuilding industry in Turkey are not available as is clear from the above table. However, there have been various long and short term loans from other countries from time to time. The most recent long term loan for the Turkish shipbuilding industry is a Japanese loan. The agreement for the loan from Japan, totaling US$ 250 million, was signed in March 1995 to be available starting from the beginning of the summer of 1996. The main targets of this loan are newbuildings of approximately 300-350 thousand dwt of ships in Turkish shipyards and to modernise Turkish shipyards using a range of Japanese technology, as noted earlier (Drewry, 1995).

Table 45
Comparison of the subsidies for the shipbuilding industry in the world and in Turkey

	in the world	in Turkey
Official subsidy	9-26%	10% + V.A.T.
Hidden subsidy	available	not available
Long term loans	available	not available
Exchange rate-actual rate difference	not available	available
Warranty	based on project	property, land, vessel
Specialised banks	available	not available

Source: Chamber of Shipping (1995c).

119

The shipyards

Turkish shipyards can be categorised in the following way:

Shipyards that belong to the Navy.
State owned shipyards that belong to the Turkish Ship Industry
Company.
Shipyards that belong to the private sector.

Naval shipyards

These shipyards are quite different from others deriving from their duties to
the defence sector. General functions are maintaining the attack and auxiliary
ships of the fleet in active service, constructing war and auxiliary ships and
equipment, supplying necessary technical services for shore facilities,
designing and producing any type of spare parts, machinery for ships and
shore facilities, and finally supplying excess capacity to the private sector for
shipbuilding, repairing, docking and technical services.

The Turkish Navy owns and operates three shipyards - Golcuk and Taskizak
shipyards in the Marmara region and Izmir shipyard in the Aegean region, of
which Golcuk shipyard at present is the most important shipbuilding unit in
Turkey in competition with others in the Eastern Mediterranean. In these
yards, submarines, destroyers, tankers or bulk material ships up to 30,000 dwt
can be built, repaired and overhauled by qualified engineers, utilising
sophisticated and modern specialist and machine tools. Total output and steel
processing at these shipyards amounts to 40,000 dwt/year and 13,000
tons/year respectively, with a total of 54,500 tons of docking capacity
(Chamber of Shipping, 1997).

Shipyards owned by the Turkish Ship Industry Company

There are five ship yards that belong to the Turkish Ship Industry Company,
which is a state owned and operated company. These are the Halic, Camialti,
Istinye and Pendik shipyards in Istanbul and the Alaybey shipyard in Izmir.
Additionally, there is an engine manufacturing plant which produces diesel
engines under a Sulzer licence at the Pendik shipyard. This latter shipyard is
the largest shipyard within the heavy industrial part of the Turkish sector.
Total newbuilding capacity within all these shipyards is around 177,900
dwt/year with a steel processing capacity of 42,077 tons/year. The Pendik

shipyard is the largest of all with a handling capacity of 75,000 dwt vessels. Outside of the shipyards in Istanbul, the Alaybey shipyard is the only one situated in Izmir in the Aegean region and mostly focuses either upon the newbuilding of small vessels and tugboats, or activities within the ship repair sector.

Private shipyards

There are a total of 40 private shipyards in Turkey with 37 of them situated within the Tuzla shipyard area in the Marmara region to the northwest of Turkey and the remaining three within the Black Sea region to the north of the country. The number of these shipyards has increased rapidly with the increased subsidies and support made available during the beginning of the 1980s. However, because of the bottleneck in shipbuilding credits after 1985, the imbalanced and unstable Turkish economy caused unemployment in the private sector shipyards, with many of the Tuzla shipyards not completing their investment programmes and never reaching the agreed capacities. On the other hand, after the 1990s, some increases in the total output of newbuildings were seen in private sector shipyards mostly based upon the dynamism, independence and entrepreneurship of this part of the industry. Total newbuilding output produced in these shipyards was 117,000 dwt in 1996 and 179,000 dwt in 1997 (Chamber of Shipping, 1998a) including general cargo vessels, tankers, multipurpose vessels, container vessels and ro-ro vessels. It was planned to produce a total output of 175,000 dwt in 1998. These private shipyards are represented by the Association of Shipbuilding Industrialists, which was established in 1971.

Current situation in the shipyards

Shipbuilding in Turkish shipyards has been carried out using some relatively up to date technology but many of the shipyards have not yet reached the highest international standards. Today, the sector remains imbalanced and unstable as a consequence of the credit conditions and inefficient subsidies that have been available and also because of the variable demand for new shipbuilding caused by the parallel variability in the situation for second-hand ship imports.

The main potential customers for Turkish shipyards are either from the Turkish domestic shipping industry or from a number of countries such as Denmark, the Netherlands, the United Kingdom, Italy and Germany. For example, Marmara Transport Shipyard has constructed river/sea-going tankers for the Russian Federation, the Sedef Shipyard has constructed various types of vessels for the Russian Federation as well and also a series of river/sea-going tankers for Azerbaijan and cargo vessels and chemical carriers for Germany and Norway. Meanwhile, Madenci Shipyard has produced a series of vessels for Denmark (Lloyd's Ship Manager, 1994). In the meantime, shipyards in China, Japan, South Korea and western Europe, which are supported by state incentives, and in Romania, Bulgaria, the Russian Federation and Poland, which are supported by both financial and technical incentives, are considered to be the main competitors (Interview, 1998b).

Table 46 illustrates the total output capacities of the state owned and private shipyards in Turkey. It is clear from the same table that the shipyards owned and operated by the private sector have double the output capacity compared with the state owned and operated shipyards. With regards to the total capacities of Turkish shipyards belonging to both private sector and the state, the total utilised capacities are approximately 10% for those state owned - leaving around 90% of the capacities of these shipyards unused. However, these percentages are very different for private shipyards where it increases to approximately 80% total utilisation for most of them.

Table 46
Output capacities of state owned and private shipyards in Turkey

Sector	Total number of shipyards	Capacity of steel processing (tons/year)	Total output capacity (dwt/year)
State	5	42,077	177,900
Private	40	138,000	410,000
TOTAL	**45**	**180,077**	**587,900**

Source: Chamber of Shipping, 1998a.

The ship repair industry in Turkey has been under rapid development and growth similar to many other industries in the country. The Tuzla Yards near Istanbul have also upgraded their repair capabilities with the recent arrival of a number of floating docks, in particular a very large one of 350 metres length, from the Port of genoa in Italy. The yards in Turkey are mostly in competition with those in Greece and Italy in the Mediterranean and Black Sea ship repair markets.

Privatisation in the Turkish shipbuilding industry

Privatisation actions in the maritime sector since the beginning of the 1990s, have focused upon the state owned ports, shipyards and the Turkish Cargo Lines Company that operates various cargo vessels. It was realised that most of the legal problems of privatisation will be overcome by minimising bureaucratic delays that were likely to occur during the Government share issues. Additionally, it was also highly recommended by the Chamber of Shipping that the state owned ports and shipyards should be privatised with immediate effect. Therefore, privatisation of the major state owned shipyards belonging to the Turkish Ship Industry Company has become one of the most important items within the Turkish privatisation process. The main target has been to convert these state owned shipyards, which have been heavily subsidised by the Government over many years, into profitable private companies. The main problems of the Turkish shipbuilding industry that this process of privatisation is expected to resolve can be listed as follows:

Problems caused by general political interference in the shipbuilding industry.

Declining demand for new shipbuilding.

Declining utilisation of these shipyards, and therefore increasing overcapacity of the yards due to the declining number of newbuildings.

Various problems related to ship repair.

Required improvements in shipbuilding technology.

Lack of financial support for the industry.

The significant rises in the costs and prices of newbuildings as a result of the high inflation rate in Turkey.

The misapplication of many loans and subsidies.

The very slow action taken by the Turkish Government in the privatisation of state owned shipyards.

The absence of any marketing strategies for the shipyards.

In order to solve these problems, the first step that has been considered consists of taking a number of immediate actions, which were noted in the Seventh Five-Year Development Plan. The most crucial of these affects the privatisation of state owned shipyards and giving them active support in restructuring them to increase their output capacity to match the dynamism characteristic of the private sector.

As a consequence, the shipbuilding industry has played and continues to play an important role in the Turkish maritime sector through its contribution to the broad economy. The annual production capacity of the Turkish shipbuilding industry with its present production techniques and technology is approximately 500,000 dwt per year or 180,000 tons of steel processing in a year. Additionally, the annual ship repair capacity of the industry is approximately seven million dwt at present. With the enlargement of capacity at Um Shipyard, the total capacity of the shipyards will reach approximately 730,000 dwt/year. In order to utilise the total capacity of the shipyards and thus decrease the amount of overcapacity, certain actions need to be taken. The most important ones were already planned by the Seventh Five-Year Development Plan for the period between 1995 and 1999 and are noted here:

It is highly recommended that the actions mentioned in this plan should be achieved as a first step.
Privatisation actions should also be speeded up by the Government.
The technologies together with the substructures of the shipyards should be improved.
Subsidies by the Government should be of a pro-active nature and speed-up the process of reform and improvement.

When the machinery and equipment used in the shipbuilding and maintenance sectors are considered, an efficient and effective component industry to feed these sectors is a vital requirement. This would be an important addition to the economy of the country but is sadly lacking at present. As a result, the direction and quantity of subsidies needs to be reviewed and the demand for domestic new shipbuilding and the potential for exports must be increased. Meanwhile, the annual new shipbuilding demand in the years 1995 to 2000 has been estimated to be double the annual average of 1998 which will increase the total tonnage from 10 million dwt to 15 million dwt by the end of the century.

The annual financial requirement in Turkey created by the scrapping of old ships has been estimated as around US$ 100 million. In addition to this, there is another financial requirement which is for second-hand ship purchase. The annual financial requirement for this purpose in Turkey is estimated as around US$ 250 million. As a result, the Turkish shipbuilding industry needs a total of US$ 500 million investment each year - US$ 150 million for newbuildings, US$ 100 million for scrapping and US$ 250 million for second-hand ship purchase, during this period of the Seventh Five-Year Development Plan, and to achieve its targets for the industry.

As previously indicated, the shipbuilding industry is highly dependent upon the secondary shipbuilding sector as an auxiliary industry. Therefore, any calculation of the volume of employment cannot be limited to the number of workers employed directly within the shipyards. Nevertheless, considering the level of domestic industrial contribution to the shipyards' activities which amounts to nearly 40-50%, it is probable that every employee in the shipbuilding industry in Turkey creates employment for around three people in the secondary shipbuilding supply industry. In the light of the discussion above, it is quite possible that Turkey will reach the targets that were noted earlier e.g. a foreign exchange substitution of US$ 1.2 billion/year, a net amount of prospective foreign exchange input (the difference between export and import values) of US$ 600 million/year, volume of employment of 105 million man-hour/year, and state revenues (employees' income taxes, premiums and other deductions plus interest on the foreign exchange substitutes) of US$ 340 million/year.

As a consequence, the achievements of the proposals contained within the Seventh Five-Year Development Plan can be summarised as follows:

newbuilding capacity: 1,000,000 dwt/year;
repair capacity : 7,500,000 dwt/year;
foreign exchange substitutes: US$ 1.5 billion/year;
employment (secondary shipbuilding industry included): 125 million man-hour/year;
domestic contribution: 65%.

Achievement of these desired targets will only be possible with the implementation of the measures proposed as a whole. The main points of the proposals are as follows:

privatisation of state owned shipyards;
extended maritime training and research;
measures for supporting both individual projects and marketing strategies;
measures for supporting investments in infrastructure;
various incentives;
activating measures.

These are the minimum measures that need to be taken by the industry if progress is to be made. If these specific proposals and recommendations are taken and put into action, then the contribution of the shipbuilding industry to the Turkish maritime sector will almost inevitably increase. Further to this it needs to be noted there has been and will continue to be a fundamental impact by the private sector within the shipbuilding industry in Turkey, as it increasingly dominates the total work of Turkish shipyards.

The scrapping industry

The term "scrapping" or "demolition" as applied to a ship means that the hull, main engines and superstructure of a vessel are dismantled when the vessel's value in conventional operational terms is considered to have been lost. As a result of this, the body of a vessel can no longer be considered as a ship and conventionally it will be used for a different purpose in the recycled steel industry as scrapped materials (Nagatsuka, 1989). For statistical purposes, the final disposition of a vessel and its registration become nullified. The average age of a vessel for scrapping is normally considered approximately 30 years. The ship scrapping industry is linked with both the shipbuilding industry and the steel industry as it plays an intermediate role between these two sectors. Approximately 200 vessels are scrapped each year.

The process of ship scrapping consists of a complex interrelationship between the shipowner, shipbroker, shipbreaker, steelmaker, the buyer of non-ferrous materials and the recycler (Drewry, 1996). Shipbreakers in particular, are working for the steel market in general because they are responsible for breaking and scrapping vessels and the sale of the resulting materials to steel companies. The various components of vessels which are recycled after scrapping include the steel plates of the hull and vessel pipes which are melted down and rolled into sheets. Aluminium equipment, deck cables and copper wire are also recycled. In addition, cranes, generators, engine and cabin materials are commonly sold for future use. It is noted by Drewry (1996) that some 30% of the steel is recycled and reused again in the future.

Factors affecting an increase or decrease in the volume of ship scrapping can be listed as follows:

Age of vessel.
General condition of the vessel (i.e. ageing, corrosion, abrasion).
Increase in repair/maintenance.
Design and efficiency of current ship size.

Decline in the efficiency of the main engine.
Regulations requiring that vessels conform to IMO and national laws.
The freight market.
Historical performance and profitability in recent years.
Future prospects.
Trade patterns.
Vessel prices/scrapping prices.
Shippers' demand.
Operational development.
Political factors.
(Nagatsuka, 1989; Drewry, 1996).

The shipping industry has reached a point where high volumes of prospective demolition candidates with large numbers of vessels in the world fleet have developed. Recent developments with advanced technologies in the ship scrapping industry have been used in some places; however, unsophisticated beach operations with 1980s' technologies still continue in many places. The major ship scrapping locations in the world were the USA, Italy, Spain and Portugal until the mid 1980s, China, South Korea and Taiwan between 1984 and 1988 and India, Pakistan and Bangladesh between 1989 and 1996. Major ship scrapping countries since the mid 1990s have tended to be Taiwan, Thailand, China, South Korea, India, Pakistan, Bangladesh, Turkey, Italy and Spain with India, Pakistan and Bangladesh, in particular (Drewry, 1996). In addition, Turkey has a distinct place in the market as the major location in the Mediterranean area. South Eastern Asia is forecast as the major ship scrapping region in the world after 1997 and into the beginning of the 2000s.

Aliaga yards in Turkey

Turkey is a major manufacturer of steel and therefore, has shown a serious interest in the scrapping industry for recycled material in steel production. Hence, this country has been one of the ship scrapping countries in the world since the late 1980s. The scrap consumption of Turkey doubled and reached nine million tonnes in 1994, from a figure which was 4.5 million tonnes in 1989 (Drewry, 1996). Today, Turkey shares 3% of world scrap consumption and is likely to remain one of the most significant countries in Europe in this market.

Aliaga yards, situated to the north of the centre of Izmir on the Aegean Sea and to the west of the country, are the only locations for the ship scrapping industry in Turkey since the 1980s. Aliaga yards have commonly been preferred as a location to scrapping small and medium size vessels either in the Far East or Southeast Asia, as it is the major scrapping centre in whole of the greater Mediterranean area. 11% of the scrapped material is used as recycled material in the steel manufacturing industry in Turkey whilst the majority of the raw materials are either imported from other countries or some supplied as wastes from other industries in the country (Chamber of Shipping, 1998a). In addition, a value added contribution to the economy results arising from scrapping old vessels and recycling their metal for the steel manufacturing industry rather than direct imports of raw materials for the same industry. Approximately, 80% of the manufacturers in the iron-steel manufacturing industry in the Aegean region use raw material received from the scrapping industry, in their recycling process. Therefore, the scrapping industry retains an important place in the contribution to the Turkish national economy.

Although the ship scrapping industry positively contributes to the economy, a number of problems are also caused by this industry. Environmental problems that arise as a result of ship scrapping are the most important ones because of the dangerous situations for both human health and the environment. Recent methods used during the process of ship scrapping have been limited by environmental concerns. Because demand for steel is good, methods used for this process which could be to the good of the environment are not taken into consideration by shipbreakers. For example, some materials and chemicals used for ship scrapping are recommended by the World Health Organisation (WHO) and International Labour Organisation (ILO) of the United Nations (UN) to be banned; however, they are still used in many countries including Turkey.

The beach method as a conventional approach to scrapping, has been used in the Aliaga yards and therefore, various environmental problems have on occasion arisen in the area. Most of the problems centre around marine and soil pollution and human diseases and a number of deaths caused by asbestos. Research was undertaken by a number of groups from the European Union and universities in Turkey since the beginning of the 1990s, resulting in conclusions that the air is commonly highly polluted with asbestos fibres and therefore, workers in this business are likely to severely affected directly by a range of lung diseases and cancer (Lorber and Loffler, 1992).

The world's environment must be considered rather than only local environmental interests and new technologies and methodologies should be applied for a more effective, efficient, economic and productive industry. Consequently, human health and human life should be the most important criteria in the ship scrapping industry, but both are currently, frequently damaged as a result of people working in this sector in Turkey. Therefore, the development of advanced technologies in this industry requires support from the Turkish government and the generation of hazardous materials caused by the scrapping industry - asbestos, in particular - require bans by regulatory institutions.

7. Turkish shipping policy: recent issues

Introduction

Turkish shipping policy consists of both international and domestic policies. International shipping policies include those which relate to the European Union maritime sector and the potential needs and requirements for accession, policies for flagging out and the development of an international ship registry, policies in connection with problems over the Turkish straits, the ISM Code, policies relating to the six mile continental shelf in the Aegean Sea, and a series of issues to do with international shipping conferences and agreements. Furthermore, domestic shipping policies include the establishment of a Ministry of Shipping, the improvement of the Turkish merchant fleet, privatisation of all parts of the industry, cabotage, financial policy, maritime education and training and the protection of environment.

International shipping policies

Relations with the European Union

Relationships between Turkey and the European Union have existed since the foundation of the latter in the late 1950s. Turkey has attempted several times to be allotted membership of the Union; however, further evaluation of membership has been suspended at present until the economy is stabilised and various problems related to human rights, self-expression and the difficulties in Turkish and Greek relations over Cyprus are resolved. Meanwhile, there has continued a general policy for improving relations with the EU in the broad field of both economics and politics. As a result of this, a Customs Union between Turkey and the EU came into effect on the 1st of January 1996 and Turkey has become one of the few non-member countries which has such an extensive arrangement of this type and extent with the EU.

As a result of Customs Union, economic relations between Turkey and the EU have increased and as an inevitable consequence, the shipping industry has been affected if only because approximately 90% of Turkish foreign trade depends upon seaborne trade. Thus, a policy supporting an increase in economic relations between Turkey and the EU has direct impact upon the shipping industry. Furthermore, another strand of this policy is to maintain the rights of Turkey to continue protected and undisturbed competition with the EU in the maritime sector, whilst maintaining relations with third countries and sharing world markets including that of the EU (Chamber of Shipping, 1995b).

Flagging out and the international second ship registry

In a similar fashion to various European Union shipowners, the Turkish shipowners clearly prefer to flag out using off-shore registries for the benefits of low taxation and crew costs. The flagged out vessels operated by the Turkish operators are approximately half of the national merchant fleet and are mostly under various flags, such as Malta, Panama, Liberia, the Bahamas or St. Vincent and the Grenadines. As a result of flagging out, an increasing freight payment to foreign flag vessels of approximately US$ 1.5 billion is lost annually.

Turkish shipowners and ship operators have been looking forward to the introduction of a Turkish international ship registry as a second registry for Turkish flagged vessels with the advantage of reduced taxation and operating costs particularly in terms of crewing. Some examples of forms of second international registry that may be adopted in Turkey have been introduced in Norway, Denmark and the UK Isle of Man. A policy for an international ship registry has been discussed so that it will act as a second registry and a flag of convenience for Turkey both for preventing the substantial loss of freight payments to overseas flagged vessels and to allow the operation of a vessel within Turkish cabotage trading. This policy has also been strongly supported by the Turkish Chamber of Shipping (Chamber of Shipping, 1995b; Undersecretariat of Shipping, 1997) because of the benefits of low taxation, similar to the situation in other countries such as Spain (Coto-Millan, 1996), low crew costs and bonus supports from the government.

The Chairman of the Chamber of Shipping in Turkey in 1997 (Mr. Kaptanoglu), noted that the second ship registry of Turkey will also be open for the registration of vessels which are under foreign flags and which will give these vessels the benefit of carrying some (Turkish) national cargo. Accordingly, it is anticipated that the share of the vessels operating under Turkish flag within the merchant fleet will increase after the introduction of the Turkish international second ship registry in addition to receiving greater revenues from the registration of vessels operating under foreign flags.

The progress of the law has been slow but by early 1998 it had reached the stage of approval by the Turkish Grand National Assembly, effectively the Turkish Parliament (The World, 1998b). The law consists of items related to types of vessels that can be registered under this registry, the types of certificates required to be kept on these vessels, nationality and employment of seamen, social security and working conditions of seamen, regulations relating to the entrance and exit of foreign seamen to and from Turkey, insurance of ships and some financial issues i.e. taxation, mortgage, leasing, foreign exchange rates, etc.

The Turkish straits

The straits of Bosphorus and Dardanelles and the Sea of Marmara in the northwest of Turkey are known as the Turkish straits where the European and Asian continents meet together. In addition, the Black Sea meets the Aegean Sea through these straits, where Turkey and Greece have coastlines, after which it meets the Mediterranean Sea. Therefore, the Turkish straits play an inevitable and important role in the geopolitical, geographical and strategic situation of Turkey.

Although the territory of these straits belongs to Turkey, the water running through them and connecting the Black Sea and the Aegean Sea is considered international waters for the purposes of freedom of navigation according to most authorities (Lloyd's List, 1997a). However, at the same time, the water running through the Turkish straits is also a domestic territory within Turkey with freedom of navigation according to the regulations brought by the Convention of Montreux, which was signed in 1936 (Lloyd's List, 1997b). Therefore, there is the freedom of passage for any type of vessel under any flag; however, it is noted by the Turkish authorities that freedom of passage does not mean uncontrolled passage.

Enormous increases in maritime traffic with a particular growth in dangerous tanker traffic, has caused problems as a result of collisions in this area, located at one point virtually within the metropolitan city of Istanbul with a population of 13 million (Lloyd's List, 1997a). For instance, an annual total of 60 million tonnes of crude oil is carried by vessels through these straits (Oguzulgen and Erol, 1997). In addition to the regulations agreed by IMO in 1994, the Turkish Government needs to establish a physical and functional substructure to control shipping movements. The Government has given approval to set up a radar traffic monitoring system covering the straits to ensure navigational safety and it is a policy of the Government to improve current regulations used for the pilotage services in this area (Undersecretariat of Shipping, 1997). At present, only Turkish vessels are obliged to have pilotage or inform the authorities during their passage through the straits. In addition to this, the Turkish authorities also try to insist upon foreign vessels having a pilotage service for safety and environmental reasons within the straits but commonly without success.

It has been suggested by IMO that an international committee should be established to find a solution to the problem of dangerous traffic in the straits. However, the Turkish authorities object to the idea of an international group deciding upon regulations for the straits because this trade route through the Turkish straits is domestic water under the sovereign control of Turkey with guaranteed freedom of passage (Lloyd's List, 1997b). Furthermore, the Turkish authorities introduced a number of additional regulations in 1994 including increased safety requirements in the straits regarding Article 24 of the Convention of Montreux. In addition, the Turkish authorities are planning to bring in another regulation that requires tankers to be covered with unlimited insurance against possible damages to third parties while passing through the straits. This problem has not yet been resolved and requires urgent solution to meet the problems of the dangerous international maritime traffic in the straits.

The ISM Code

The ISM Code is essentially the documentation of an International Management Code for the Safe Operation of Ships and Pollution Prevention aimed to assist in compliance with the IMO Conventions and the Preservation of Life and the Environment. The regulation was adopted on the 4th November 1993 by the IMO and was amended as a section to SOLAS-74 in May 1994 (Cowley, 1995; Kolay, 1995) with the main aim of preventing casualties and marine pollution. The ISM Code defines the safety management system and responsibilities for the shipping industry in addition to IMO

Guidelines for administration and implementation of the ISM Code. Therefore, the ISM Code has become a mandatory regulation and a required process of certification, which ensures a clear definition and documentation of policies, responsibilities, procedure guidelines and job titles.

The implementation dates for the ISM Code are dependent upon the type of vessels, i.e. 1st July 1998 for passenger ships and passenger high speed craft, tankers, bulk carriers and cargo high speed craft up to 500 grt; 1st July 2002 for other cargo vessels up to 500 grt and mobile off-shore drilling units; 1st July 2006 for all vessels between 150-500 grt. In addition, implementation of the ISM Code came into effect on 1st July 1996 for passenger ships in EU countries (Cowley, 1995) and companies operating passenger ships and ferries to and from EU countries became subject to auditing from this date (Official Journal of the EC, 1995). It should be noted that successful implementation of the Code depends upon the commitment of the companies, the attitude of the auditors and co-operation between these parties if a significant contribution to maritime safety and pollution prevention is to be achieved.

Inevitably, the implementation of the ISM Code for passenger ships and ferries in the EU has had a direct impact upon ferry services between Turkey and the EU in the major market of the Eastern Mediterranean including those vessels operated by Turkish operators. In parallel to the regulations brought by the ISM Code, the Undersecretariat of Shipping in Turkey also issued a regulation in 1996, requiring a Line Permit for international ferry services, particularly in the Italy-Greece-Turkey corridor where the total number of passengers has rapidly increased after the civil war in the former Yugoslavia from the beginning of the 1990s. A number of regulations had to be adopted because of various problems faced by passengers in this corridor in previous years. The aim of this permit is to improve the quality of ferry services and standards of ferries and prepare the quality of these vessels for the ISM Code. The certificates required by a ferry to operate a service on an international line are those of register, tonnage, seaworthiness, international oil pollution prevention, load line, passenger ship safety, minimum safe manning, radio and telephone regulations, apparatus manufacturer and maintenance, and hygienic conditions (Undersecretariat of Shipping, 1996).

In addition to the ferry services between Turkey and the EU, Turkish cargo shipping and tanker operations will also be considerably affected following the implementation of the ISM Code on 1st July 1998 with cargo vessels and operating companies becoming subject to audit. Moreover, it is strictly stated by the IMO that cargo vessels and tankers should have met the ISM Code requirements by the date noted earlier - 1st July 1998 - which caused various problems for many Turkish operators because many were very unlikely to be ready in time.

Six mile continental shelf in the Aegean Sea

Although Greece and Turkey are NATO allies, there has been a form of 'cold war' between them for many years. Greece has stated its intention to claim the full 12-mile maritime boundary from time to time, by supporting international maritime regulations for its islands and approximately 1000 rocky islets in the Aegean Sea (Lloyd's List, 1996a; Lloyd's List, 1996b). On the other hand, the policy of Turkey has been to support a special agreement for a six mile continental shelf in the Aegean Sea to protect Turkish cabotage trade (Fairplay, 1994; Chamber of Shipping, 1996b).

Policy for international conferences and agreements

Turkey is a member of the Organisation of Economic Co-operation and Development (OECD). The Maritime Transport Committee of the OECD was established in 1961 and deals with relations and problems in the maritime industry, between the member countries and between the member countries and third countries. Turkey is also a member of UNCTAD within the group of OECD members. In addition, Turkey agreed and signed the conventions of SOLAS 1974 and STCW 1978 of the International Maritime Organisation (IMO).

Turkish representatives from the maritime sector and ship operators and shipowners in particular, want their voices to be heard in the world maritime sector. It has been noted by the Turkish maritime authorities that one way of achieving this is to participate in international maritime conferences and agreements.

Consequently, international shipping policies towards flagging out and the creation of an international ship registry, towards the Turkish straits and the ISM Code appear to be more important policies than many others because of their crucial effects upon Turkish shipping in the international arena. Details of the importance of these policies will be discussed in the concluding section of this discussion.

Domestic shipping policies

Establishment of a Ministry of Shipping

Maritime affairs are controlled by various ministries in Turkey. For example, the main ports are owned and operated by Turkish State Railways, which is under the responsibility of the Ministry of Transport whilst other activities are the responsibility of the Shippinmg Undersecretariat of the Prime Ministry. Various problems commonly arise because of bureaucracy and the spread of responsibility between the ministries and lack of communication between various authorities. As a consequence, there is a widely recognised need for the establishment of a single Ministry of Shipping to control maritime affairs under one main authority.

Policy for the improvement of the Turkish merchant fleet

This policy is mainly concerned with the technological improvement, modernisation and development of the Turkish merchant fleet to a total of 20 million dwt by the beginning of 2000 from 10.89 million dwt at the end of 1996. It is currently the plan that the Turkish merchant fleet will be placed within the first ten countries in the world by the year 2000, from its position of 17th in 1996 as noted earlier. It has also an ambition to reduce the average age of the fleet to 15 years and to modernise and upgrade the fleet by building new vessels by that same year. The contribution of the shipping industry to the national economy is approximately US$ 6 billion per year at present and is planned to have risen to approximately US$ 10 billion by the beginning of 2000.

In addition, there are a number of other issues, which have also been adopted under this policy. These include the encouragement of the use of shipping in inland waterways, the increase of the share of vessels under Turkish flag within seaborne foreign trade and the construction of more container vessels and terminals to match the increases in the demand for container shipping that are anticipated. Moreover, it has also been a policy to encourage shipping and trading in inland waterways in the Black Sea countries stemming from the increasing seaborne trade as a direct impact of the Black Sea Economic Co-operation.

Privatisation

Since the beginning of the 1990s, a number of proposals have been made for privatisation of various state owned institutions within a number of sectors, including the maritime sector. Some steps have been taken under these privatisation actions and some institutions have been privatised. However, various state owned institutions in the maritime sector are still under privatisation action waiting to be privatised.

The Turkish Maritime Organisation regularly makes heavy losses of more than US$ 20 billion each year with an excess capacity and over employment of more than 3000 people, the majority working for city passenger services. Suborganisations of the Turkish Maritime Organisation are included within the privatisation programme and have been subject to privatisation actions since the beginning of the 1990s. This organisation covers the operation of various ports, the national carrier Turkish Cargo Lines, and the national ro-ro and passenger ferry operator Turkish Maritime Lines as noted earlier.

In particular, the Turkish national carrier Turkish Cargo Lines, was selected first for privatisation as a result of achieving a US$ 8 million profit in 1993 after several years of loss (Seatrade Review, 1993). Turkish Cargo Lines, has a preference agreement for carrying Turkish military and other government cargoes that are mainly from western Europe and the USA - 50% of government cargoes must be carried by Turkish flag vessels. Turkish Maritime Lines, which is the main ro-ro and passenger ferry operator, operates national passenger ferry services, city passenger services, international ro-ro services in the Black Sea and international passenger ferry services in the Eastern Mediterranean, in the Italy-Greece-Turkey corridor.

Turkish State Railways operates the seven major ports in Turkey and privatisation action is in progress including the biggest container terminals at the Ports of Istanbul, Izmir and Mersin. In addition, privatisation of the twelve secondary ports owned and operated by the Turkish Maritime Organisation is also in line. It is noted that privatisation of these ports would prevent monopolisation, whilst competition between the ports would reduce costs and improve service quality. Although the ports are not privatised yet, port tariffs of some ports have been freed up since 1995 (Seatrade Review, 1995).

The major four shipyards in Turkey are state owned and operated by Turkish Shipbuilding Industry (TSI) and are currently under privatisation action. The potential capacity of the shipyards is considered as a minimum of 1 million dwt per year. However, many shipyards in Turkey utilise only 10% of their capacity. The output of the Turkish shipyards was approximately 68,000 grt in the mid 1980s, representing 2% of the total West European merchant ship building output (Drewry, 1995). Losses were US$73 million in 1992 and US$31 million in 1993 and it is widely considered that productivity and efficiency at shipyards could have been better. The shipbuilding industry has been partially subsidised by state funds. New building orders were particularly from shipowners of Poland, Germany, Norway, the UK and the Netherlands. Additionally, new buildings have also continued for Turkish shipowners.

Cabotage

Trading between Turkish ports is controlled by the law of cabotage, dated the 13th April 1926, and is part of the general body of Turkish Trade Law. Turkey has great potential for cabotage shipping because of its long coastline of approximately 8000 kilometres. However, cabotage shipping continues to suffer and lose its economic place within the overall Turkish shipping market largely because of the inefficiencies of the monopoly held by the state owned cargo carrier and the failure thus to complete effectively with trucking as an alternative mode.

Financial policy

Approximately 60% of investment in the maritime sector in Turkey is covered through capital of the shipping companies. Meanwhile government subsidy in the maritime sector is approximately 10%, in general terms. A variety of loans and credits are used by shipping companies at their own risk. The most recent and significant loan of a total of US$ 250 million was borrowed from Japan and was backed by a guarantee of the Turkish Treasury (Lloyd's List, 1997a).

In addition, it has been agreed to establish a specialised bank in the maritime sector or an International Consortium Bank by International banks and Turkish shipowners to match the financial demand for new investment, new shipbuilding, technological improvement and modernisation of the merchant fleet and to solve financial problems related to these areas. Similar banks which are specialised in shipping, are already in business in some countries, such as Japan, Korea, Sweden and Norway. Furthermore, a number of items have also been adopted recently by the Government, such as the establishment of a maritime foundation, easing bureaucratic problems for leasing and operating vessels under Turkish flags during the period of the lease, and the opening up of shipping company activities to public scrutiny.

Maritime education and training

The main purpose of maritime education and training is to increase the safety, functioning and economics of maritime activities, thus reducing the cost of sea transportation and to improve the conditions of competition and co-operation with other transportation systems. Therefore, maritime education and training have significance at Government level. A number of factors, such as achieving the STCW standards and IMO and ILO recommendations, the basic Law of National Education and the regulations of the Ministry of National Education and the requirements of the Turkish Higher Education Authority, are currently significant for maritime education and training in Turkey.

The Turkish Maritime Education Foundation was established in 1993 and a considerable number of donations were collected from ship owners, ship operators and maritime companies. The main goal of the Foundation is to train seamen and people related to the maritime industry through sandwich courses and seminars and to provide certain facilities and laboratories to the maritime schools.

There are 13 maritime high schools, a number of maritime departments at various universities and a limited number of postgraduate programmes with very few shipping related academics mostly situated in Istanbul and Izmir (Undersecretariat of Shipping, 1997). This provision is considered very little in terms of matching the high potential of the needs of maritime education in Turkey. Despite the importance given by the Government to maritime education and training, it is widely considered that the Government gives insufficient attention to the newly established maritime schools at the universities through insufficient subsidies.

Protection of the environment

This policy, which was recently officially adopted, covers the establishment of treatment plants at ports, supporting the construction of sewerage systems in metropolitan cities for the protection of the seas and meeting the requirements of international conventions for the prevention of marine pollution caused by vessels (Chamber of Shipping, 1997). This policy is actively supported by the Association of Clean Seas in Turkey.

Overall, domestic shipping policies for the establishment of the Ministry of Shipping, improvement of the merchant fleet, privatisation and improvement of maritime education and training are generally considered to be the most important ones. Their importance will be stressed in the following concluding section of this part of the text.

Conclusions and discussion of Turkish shipping policies

Regarding both the international and national maritime policies of Turkey, most continue to remain only promises of the Government. Ship operators, shipowners and ship builders complain about excessive bureaucracy in Turkey, particularly with regards to privatisation actions since the beginning of the 1990s as noted earlier. After reviewing all the maritime policies of Turkey, it is necessary now to note the most significant ones that have specific impacts upon the maritime industry.

Policies for flagging out and creating an international ship registry, those relating to the Turkish straits and also those for the ISM Code appear to be the most significant ones at the international level because they require urgent solutions at present. The increasing seaborne traffic has been a significant issue for safety and environmental pollution prevention in the Turkish straits as noted earlier. The Turkish Government should take further urgent steps to develop solutions, which are based upon the requirements of law and conventions at the international level. In a similar fashion to various European Union shipowners for instance, a number of Turkish shipowners clearly prefer to flag out using off-shore registries to realise the benefits of low taxation and crew costs.

Further significant stress needs to be given to the ISM Code by Turkish shipowners and ship operators because the certification for this Code has come into force early in the EU in mid 1998. Moreover, approximately half of Turkish seaborne foreign trade is conducted to and from European Union countries; however, only a few Turkish shipowners and ship operators have either met or even applied to match the requirements of the certificate of this Code. Inevitably it will be the case that Turkish shipowners and ship operators will face a considerable number of problems in the near future stemming from failing to match the requirements of the ISM Code by the required time and this issue must be highlighted both to and by the Government in terms of its potentially direct impact upon Turkish seaborne foreign trade.

The creation of a second registry for Turkish shipping will be an important stage in preventing flagging out, and in parallel to this, in increasing and protecting market share of the Turkish flag vessels for Turkish shipping. It is believed by the Turkish ship operators and shipowners that the Government can also support the industry by establishing this registry and avoiding the need to provide excessive subsidies through direct financial aids or incentives; these latter remain as promises.

In addition to these policies, the improvement and development of the Turkish merchant fleet is another significant policy for Turkey. Although it is one of the ideas for shipping policy of the Government, Turkish shipowners and ship operators do not receive direct subsidies nor financial aid from the Government. On the contrary, they survive and trade on their own meeting the full requirements of Turkish liberalisation policy. A number of other subjects are to be encouraged by the Government to help with the improvement of the fleet, including those relating to inland waterway shipping, Black Sea shipping, the building of container vessels etc. However, these encouragements remain only as promises of the Government who so far have not taken any further steps in terms of either direct financial aid or indirect support. Therefore, dynamism in the private sector of the Turkish shipping industry is what makes this industry one of the most significant and locomotive industries in Turkey. As a result, improvement of the Turkish merchant fleet with an average age of 15 years, a total of 20 million dwt and a direct contribution of US$ 10 billion to the national economy are the main targets that have been adopted for the Turkish shipping industry. Privatisation will provide a direct role in achieving these targets for the industry with inevitable contributions from the privatised national carrier, national ferry operator and the major ports, in particular. In addition, the improvement of maritime education and training along with the development of current institutions is another significant issue that forms the basis of Turkish shipping policy.

Overall, the establishment of a Ministry of Shipping in Turkey will play the crucial role in achieving each of the above noted issues in the shipping industry by collecting together and covering the responsibilities and institutions under one authority. Inevitably, there are other policy issues not indicated here but those noted above are undoubtedly the most significant.

8. Conclusions and discussion

Turkey is located on both the continents of Europe and Asia and has as neighbours a number of Eastern European, Mediterranean, Middle Eastern and Former Soviet Union (CIS) countries. As such, it has a unique character much of which is derived from its geographical and strategic situation. Turkey has long been of the status of a developing country reflecting the character that this suggests upon many of its industrial sectors with moves towards rapid development and technological and efficiency improvements. Although the Turkish economy has yet to see much improvement, the development of a free market in the country following the economic liberalisation policy adopted during the beginning of the 1980s, is just beginning to reflect the dynamism of the private sector in many of the industrial sectors. A distinct and representative example of these developments exists in the shipping industry.

Approximately 90% of foreign trade in Turkey is carried by sea transport with a merchant fleet of 10.56 million dwt in late 1997 to provide for these domestic needs. The average age of the fleet totalling 1197 vessels is around 17 years, as noted earlier, and although it shows a slight decline in recent years it remains notable for its excess The Turkish merchant fleet has remained since 1992 as either the 17th or the 16th on the list of the world merchant fleet sizes.

The main driving force of the shipping industry in Turkey has been the private sector and the dynamism of the free market conditions within the liberalised economy. As also noted earlier, the majority of the major shipping

142

companies belong to the private sector with only two of the other major ones remaining state owned.

Unfortunately, there remain a number of problems with the Turkish economy, which are mainly generated by public sector activities, e.g. high inflation rates, high interest rates and the value of the Turkish Lira against hard currency. The maritime private sector has been largely immune to the unstable and uncertain economic conditions in Turkey and therefore, entrepreneurs are rapidly making decisions at their own risk and using their own resources, bolstered by access to hard currency earnings and thus are not badly affected by the situation. As a consequence it has continued to contribute positively and directly to the national economy throughout the economic traumas of the 1980s and 1990s. The industry provides an increasing financial contribution to the national economy of an approximate US$ 6 billion in 1996 and US$ 6.5 billion in 1997.

There is rapid growth in shipping and generally an increase in the development of the Turkish merchant fleet, although progress in size tends to vary year by year. A number of problems exist and require fairly immediate solution in terms of either financial or legal measures. In particular, financial sources for the maritime sector require urgent development and improvement to aid the merchant fleet. Financial leasing has been one of the growing solutions in terms of financing vessel newbuildings and various other aspects of ship operations. There is an urgent need for a bank specialised in the maritime sector to provide facilities for issuing credits or loans to the shipping industry.

The major ports - that is, the Ports of Istanbul, Izmir and Mersin - have continued to play important roles within the general international sea transport sector; however, they are operated by Turkish State Railways, controlled by the Ministry of Transport and require advanced technology investment and improvement in port efficiency. Recently developing private ports have been increasing their share in the market by placing themselves as the competitors of the state owned and operated ports in port pricing and port services, in particular.

Total output capacity of the shipbuilding industry in Turkey is approximately 500,000 dwt a year with a total 10% utilisation at major state owned shipyards. On the contrary, the same percentage reaches up to 80% in many of the private shipyards. Although annual new building capacity has been targetted at 1,000,000 dwt, unfortunately the industry remains both imbalanced and unstable as a result of credit and loan conditions and insufficient subsidy. In parallel to the shipbuilding industry, intense competition is taking place in the ship repair industry with Greek yards, for the Mediterranean market. Similarly, the scrapping industry in Turkey has a distinctive place in the same market and continues to contribute positively to the economy. However, the negative impacts upon health and the environment stemming from the traditional methods employed need to be considered and further legal regulations are needed urgently.

Some policies have been developed for the shipping industry both for the international and domestic situations. Policies for flagging out and an international ship registry, the Turkish straits and the ISM Code appear to be the most significant ones at the international level because they require urgent national and international solutions at present, which can only be decided by the Government. The ever increasing seaborne traffic has been a significant issue in terms of safety and environmental pollution prevention in the Turkish straits. The Turkish Government should take further steps to develop solutions to address these problems, which are based upon the requirements of both laws and conventions at an international and domestic level. In addition to these policies, improvement and development of the Turkish merchant fleet is another significant maritime policy with privatisation and improvement of maritime education and training adding another dimension to the range of significant shipping policies that are required.

Overall, establishment of the Ministry of Shipping in Turkey will play a crucial role in achieving these issues in the shipping industry by collecting together all the responsibilities and institutions under one ministerial roof and by providing for co-ordination between these institutions. Inevitably, there are other policy issues that could have been developed but those noted above are the most significant at present for the Turkish government to address.

Consequently, the Turkish shipping industry continues to be one of the major elements of the country's economy at present. The main reasons of its important role rest with its high hard currency earning potential and this depends largely upon the activities of the private sector and its operations within the dynamics of the market place where intense competition and a high level of entrepreneurial activity continues to take place.

References

Akyuz Y. (1989) *Financial System and Policies in Turkey in the 1980s,* UNCTAD Discussion Papers no 25, Geneva.

Association of Aegean Young Businessmen - AAYB (1995) *Economic Vision,* February, Izmir, Turkey, p.64.

Association of Independent Industrialists and Businessmen - AIIB (1996) *The Turkish Economy-1996*, Istanbul, Turkey, pp.5, 8, 27, 32, 39, 41.

Association of Turkish Industrialists and Businessmen - ATIB (1995*) Turkish Economy '95*, August, Istanbul, Turkey, pp.7-14.

Borovali O. (1997) Turmepa News, *Turkish Shipping World*, October, Chamber of Shipping Publication, Istanbul, Turkey, pp.63-64.

Buyukdeniz A. (1996) Macroeconomic expectations in the seventh five-year development plan, *Frame*, Association of Independent Industrialists and Businessmen-AIIB, 1, Istanbul, Turkey, pp.58-61.

Caki S. (1996) *Ship Investment and Finance in Ship Management*, Unpublished M.Sc. Dissertation, Dokuz Eylul University, Izmir, Turkey, pp.18-26, 42-45.

Cargo News: Transportation and Logistics (1998) May, Istanbul, Turkey, pp.1-15.

Chamber of Naval Architects (1989) *1st National Maritime Congress - Report on Naval Arcitecture Sector*, Istanbul, Turkey, pp 2-6.

Chamber of Shipping (1995a) *Report on Shipping Sector-1994*, Istanbul, Turkey, pp.97, 100, 156, 169-172, 198, 228, 244-246.

Chamber of Shipping (1995b) *Turkish Shipping at the Beginning of 1995*, Istanbul, Turkey, pp.6-8, 12, 17.

Chamber of Shipping (1995c) *Turkish and World Shipping in 1995*, Istanbul, Turkey, pp 16-18.

Chamber of Shipping (1996a) *Report on Shipping Sector-1995*, Istanbul, Turkey, pp.118, 120, 213, 242.

Chamber of Shipping (1996b) *Turkish Shipping Report*, Istanbul, Turkey, p.16.

Chamber of Shipping (1996c) *Turkish Shipping World*, January, Istanbul, Turkey, pp.9, 11-12, 15, 19.

Chamber of Shipping (1996d) *Turkish Shipping World*, April, Istanbul, Turkey, pp.40-41, 69.

Chamber of Shipping (1996e) *Turkish Shipping World*, July, Istanbul, Turkey, pp.24.

Chamber of Shipping (1996f) *Turkish Shipping World*, August, Istanbul, Turkey, pp.12, 61, 64, 66.

Chamber of Shipping (1997) *Report on Shipping Sector-1996*, Istanbul, Turkey, pp.45, 85-95.

Chamber of Shipping (1998a) *Report on Shipping Sector-1997*, Istanbul, Turkey, pp.69, 93-95, 99-101.

Chamber of Shipping (1998b) *Data Files: Top Shipowners*, Istanbul, Turkey, 10/02/98.

Chamber of Shipping (1998c) *Turkish Shipping World*, June, Istanbul, Turkey, pp.30-37.

Containerisation International (1995) February, p.83.

Coto-Millan P. (1996) Maritime Transport Policy in Spain (1974-1995), *Journal of Transport Policy*, vol. 3, no. 1/2, pp.37-41.

Cowley J. (1995) The Concept of the ISM Code, *Conference Proceedings on Management and Operation of Ships*, The Institute of Marine Engineers Press, vol. 107, no.2, London, pp.3-37.

Cruise and Ferry Info (1994) vol. 10, Marine Trading, Sweden, p.46.

Denizati (1997) New Regulations related to Ballast Waters, January-February, Istanbul, Turkey, pp.14-15.

Development Centre for the Economy - IGEME (1995) *Comparison of State Subsidies and Incentives in the European Union and Turkey*, January, Ankara, Turkey, pp.52-57.

Dorsey J. and Hindle T. (1995) Talking Turkey, *The Shield Magazine*, vol. 4, p.8.

Drewry Shipping Consultants (1995) *The Shipbuilding Market: Analysis and Forecasting of World Shipping Demand - 1995-2010*, London, pp. 37, 38, 69.

Drewry Shipping Consultants (1996) *Ship Scrapping: Locations, Activity, Price Trends and Problems*, London.

Ersoy A. and Guran N. (1993) *Turkish Economy and Expectations in 1993*, Association of Aegean Young Businessmen, Turkey, p.7.

Europe Review 1995: The Economic and Business Report (1994) eighth edition, Kogan Page and Walden Publishing, London, pp.258, 260-261.

European Commission (1996) *Short Sea Shipping*, Directorate General VII-39, Brussels, p.46.

European Marketing Pocket Book: 1994 (1995) NTC Publications Ltd., UK, pp.221-224.

Fairplay (1993) UK, 02/12/93.

Fairplay (1994) UK, 15/12/94.

Fairplay World Shipping Directory 1995-96 (1995) Fairplay Publications Ltd., UK, pp.50-71, 184-88, 306-7, 678-9, 686-87.

Financial Times (1994) Financial Times Survey: Turkey, UK, 15/04/94.

Forum (1997) A huge privatisation action on seas, February, Istanbul, Turkey, pp.40-47.

Forum (1998) Privatisation actions since 1985, April, Istanbul, Turkey, pp.20-30.

Gordon W. and Langmaid R. (1988) *Qualitative Market Research*, Gower Publishing Co. Ltd., England, pp.1-4.

Hurriyet (1996) Istanbul, Turkey, 20/10/96.

International Transport News (1996) Awards for shipping companies, September, Uzman Publications, Ankara, Turkey, p.32.

International Transport News (1998) Uzman Publications, Ankara, Turkey, pp.18, 24-28, 40-49, 54-55.

Interview (1998a) Mr Bayram Yucel - Deputy Manager, Port of Izmir, Izmir, Turkey, 02/06/98.

Interview (1998b) Mr Kenan Torlak - Chairman of Association of shipbuilding Industrialists, Turkey, 01/05/98.

ISL (1993) January-February, Bremen.

ISL (1994) January-February, Bremen.

ISL (1995) January-February, Bremen.

ISL (1996) January-February, Bremen.

ISL (1997) January-February, Bremen.

Kalpsuz T. (1980) *Shipping Law*, 1, Ankara, Turkey, pp.13-17, 51, 63.

Kazgan G. (1985) *Outward Growth in the Economy*, Istanbul, Turkey, pp.5-8.

Kender R. and Cetingil E. (1992) *Shipping Law*, 5th edition, Istanbul, Turkey, pp.13, 23-30.

Kolay O. (1995) ISM Code: A New Approach to Safety of Vessels, *Conference Proceedings on Naval Architecture and Sea Technology*, Istanbul Technical University Press, Istanbul, Turkey, 22-24/11/95, pp.1-7.

Kurdas K. (1994) *Observations on Economic Policy*, Beta Publishing, Istanbul, Turkey, p.189.

Lake M. (1996) A Historical Decision: Customs Union, *EC News*, European Commission Turkish Representative Publication, January, Ankara, Turkey, pp.1-2.

Ledger G. and Roe M. (1993) East European Shipping and Economic Change: A Conceptual Model, *Maritime Policy and Management*, 20, no.3, pp.229-241.

Ledger G. and Roe M. (1996) *East European Change and Shipping Policy*, Avebury Press, Aldershot, UK.

Lloyd's List (1994) Lloyd's of London Press Ltd., UK, 10/10/94.

Lloyd's List (1996a) Lloyd's of London Press Ltd., UK, 02/03/96.

Lloyd's List (1996b) Lloyd's of London Press Ltd., UK, 18/05/96.

Lloyd's List (1996c) Lloyd's of London Press Ltd., UK, 09/07/96.

Lloyd's List (1997a) Lloyd's of London Press Ltd., UK, 16/07/97.

Lloyd's List (1997b) Lloyd's of London Press Ltd., UK, 25/07/97.

Lloyd's Ship Manager (1993) *Turkish Shipping and Ports Directory-1993*, August, Lloyd's of London Press Ltd., UK, p.11.

Lloyd's Ship Manager (1994) *Turkish Shipping and Ports Directory-1994*, July, Lloyd's of London Press Ltd., UK, pp.7, 9, 23, 39.

Lorber K.E. and Loffler F. (1992) Asbestos Problem on Aliaga Scrapping Yards, Working Paper, Berlin.

Maddison R. (1980) *Block 2: A.Conceptual Modelling, B.Logical Modelling*, Course Team, The Open University Press, Great Britain, pp. 7, 9-11, 60.

Mersin Chamber of Shipping (1995) *Shipping Trade*, August, Mersin, Turkey, p.16.

Middle East Research Institute (1985) *Meri Report: Turkey*, University of Pennsylvania, Croom Helm Ltd., USA, pp.4-6, 8, 10.

Ministry of Labour and Social Security (1996) *Working Paper: Turkish People Living Abroad*, Ankara, Turkey.

Ministry of State (1997) *Design of Law on the Establishment of the Ministry of Shipping*, Prime Ministry Press, Ankara, Turkey, p.2.

Ministry of Transport (1992) *Shipping Law*, Sea Transport General Directorate, Ankara, Turkey, pp.179, 197, 198, 214, 227, 229, 493, 545, 552, 586.

148

Nagatsuka S. (1989) *Study about the Extension of the Scrapping Age of Tankers*, Japan Maritime Research Institute Report (JAMRI) No. 35, Japan, pp. 3, 37-62.

Nas T.F. (1992) The Impact of Turkey's Stabilisation and Structural Adjustment Programme: An Introduction, in Nas, T.F. and Odekon, M. (eds) *Economics and Politics of Turkish Liberalisation*, Associated University Presses, New Jersey, pp.11-25.

Nehir L. (1993) *Integration of Ship Industry and Defense Industry*, Undersecretariat of Defense Industry, Ankara, Turkey, p 10.

Observation (1996) Shipping Supplement, Milliyet Publications, Istanbul, Turkey, 07/10/96.

Official Journal of the European Communities - OJL (1995) No.320, 30/12/95.

Oguzulgen S. and Erol A. (1997) Current Developments on the Turkish Straits, *Shipping Trade*, Mersin Chamber of Shipping, August, Mersin, Turkey, pp.27-31.

Olali H. and Timur A. (1992) *Tourism in the Turkish Economy*, Izmir,Turkey, p.9.

Organisation for Economic Cooperation and Development - OECD (1988) *Regional Problems and Policies in Turkey*, Paris, pp.12-15.

Oyan O. (1987) *Outward Looking and Fiscal Policies in the 24-January-Economy*, Ankara, Turkey, pp.15-18, 167, 205.

Oyan O. (1989) *Outward Looking Economic and Fiscal Policies: 1980-1989*, 2nd edition, Ankara, Turkey, pp.167, 209, 225, 251, 301.

Ozturk I. (1996) Urban Substructures and Environmental Protection in the Seventh Five-Year Development Plan, *Frame*, Association of Independent Industrialists and Businessmen-AIIB, 1, Istanbul, Turkey, pp.151-155.

Parasuraman A. (1991) *Marketing Research*, 2nd edition, Addison-Wesley Publishing Co.Inc., USA, pp.252-252, 767, 882.

Sayari S. (1992) Politics and Economic Policy-Making in Turkey, 1980-1988, in Nas, T.F. and Odekon, M. (ed.s) *Economics and Politics of Turkish Liberalisation*, Associated University Presses, New Jersey, pp.26, 29.

Seatrade Review (1993) *Turkish Shipping Guide*, November, UK, p.118.

Seatrade Review (1995) July, UK, p.63.

Seatrade Review (1997) May, UK, pp.67-80.

State Institute of Statistics - SIS (1980) *Annual Statistics*, Ankara, Turkey.

State Institute of Statistics (1990) *Annual Statistics*, Ankara, Turkey.

State Institute of Statistics (1995) *Statistics and Analysis of the Turkish Economy*, Ankara, Turkey, pp.1, 199, 214-217, 322-323.

State Institute of Statistics (1996) *Annual Statistics of the Foreign Trade-1995*, Ankara, Turkey, pp.iii-xii.

State Institute of Statistics (1998) *Annual Statistics of the Foreign Trade-1997*, Ankara, Turkey.

State Planning Organisation (1996) *The Seventh Five-Year Development Plan*, Prime Ministry Press, Ankara, Turkey, pp.3-5.

Temel A. (1996)·The Seventh Five-Year Development Plan: 1996-2000, *Frame*, Association of Independent Industrialists and Businessmen-AIIB, Istanbul, Turkey, pp.30-33.

The Economist (1985) *Yearbook of Turkey-1995*, Hurriyet Publications, Istanbul, Turkey, 22/01/95, pp.68-75, 124-125.

The Secretariat of Transportation (1996) *Data Files*, Washington D.C., p.11.

The World (1997) *Shipping*, Istanbul, Turkey, 30/06/97.

The World (1998a) *Cargo and Freight Transportation*, Istanbul, Turkey, 23/02/98.

The World (1998b) *Shipping and Transportation*, Istanbul, Turkey, 26/02/98.

The World (1998c) *Shipping and Forwarding*, Istanbul, Turkey, 26/05/98.

Togan S. Olgun H. and Akder H. (1987) *Report on Developments in External Economic Relations of Turkey*, Research Centre of the Foreign Trade Association of Turkey, Ankara, pp.5, 7, 9, 43.

Turkish Cargo Lines (1998) *Data Files*, Istanbul, Turkey.

Turkish Maritime Lines (1995) *Report on Ferry Services: Italy-Turkey*, Ankara, Turkey, pp.11-13.

Turkish Maritime Organisation - TMO (1993) *Data Files*, Izmir, Turkey.

Turkish Maritime Organisation (1994) *Data Files*, Izmir, Turkey.

Turkish Maritime Organisation (1995) *Data Files*, Izmir, Turkey.

Turkish State Railways - TSR (1998) *Turkish Ports operated by TSR*, Istanbul, Turkey, pp.1-5.

Uctum M. (1992) The Effects of Liberalisation on Traded and Nontraded Goods Sectors: The Case of Turkey, in Nas T.F. and Odekon M. (eds) *Economics and Politics of Turkish Liberalisation*, Associated University Presses, New Jersey, pp.143-154.

UNCTAD (1994) Review of Maritime Transport - 1994, UNCTAD Publication, New York.

Undersecretariat of Shipping (1996) *Legislation Paper: Line Permit*, Ankara, Turkey, 25/01/96.

Undersecretariat of Shipping, (1997) *National Shipping Congress: Final Reports*, Prime Ministry Press, Ankara, Turkey, pp.164-168.

Union of Turkish Chambers (1994) *Report on the Turkish Economy*, Ankara, Turkey, p.40.

Uslu S. (1996) Social Life in the Turkish Society, *Frame*, Association of Independent Industrialists and Businessmen-AIIB, 1, Istanbul, Turkey, pp.138-140.

Uysal Y. and Mazgit I. (1996) *The Turkish Economy at the Beginning of 1996*, Association of Turkish Young Businessmen-ATYB, Izmir, Turkey, pp.13, 28.

Uygur E. (1993) *Liberalisation and Economic Performance in Turkey*, UNCTAD Discussion Paper no.65, Switzerland.

Yalcintas N. (1996) Regarding the Seventh Five-Year-Development Plan, *Frame*, Association of Independent Industrialists and Businessmen-AIIB, 1, Istanbul, Turkey, pp.39-40.

Yeni Asir (1995) Izmir, Turkey, 16/09/95.

Printed and bound by CPI Group (UK) Ltd, Croydon, CR0 4YY
08/05/2025
01864377-0002